DESIGNS
for PARKS and
RECREATION SPACES

DESIGNS
for PARKS and RECREATION SPACES

THEODORE D. WALKER, FASLA

PDA PUBLISHERS
Mesa, Arizona

Copyright ©1987 by Theodore D. Walker

Library of Congress Cataloging in Publication Data

Walker, Theodore D.
　　Designs for parks and recreation spaces.

　　Bibliography: p.
　　Includes index.
　　1. Parks — Designs and plans.　2. Parks — Pictorial
works.　3. Recreation areas — Designs and plans.
4. Recreation areas — Pictorial works.　5. Parks —
United States — Designs and plans.　6. Parks —
United States — Pictorial works.　7. Recreation areas —
United States — Designs and plans.　8. Recreation
areas — United States — Pictorial works.
9. United States — Description and travel —
1981–　　　— Views. I. Title.

SB486.D46W35　1987　　　　712'.5　　　87-2429
ISBN 0-914886-38-X
ISBN 0-914886-39-8 (pbk.)

PDA PUBLISHERS CORPORATION
1725 East Fountain
Mesa, Arizona 85203

CONTENTS

Contents continued, next page

INTRODUCTION

The main focus of this book is to present a diversity of designs for parks and recreation spaces. The presentation is in the form of a brief description for each project and some illustrations to show design intent. Some of the descriptions were written by the designers involved while the author prepared some from other sources. The illustrations include master plans, sketches, and photographs. Many of the photographs are those of the author, but some have been provided by the design firm whose project is presented.

The projects vary in scale, scope and location. There is geographic diversity. Projects range from small urban mini-parks to remote parks in very scenic settings. There are urban, suburban, waterfront, and theme parks. Included are some botanical and zoological gardens. There are a few unique parks designed for landfills, reclaimed quarries and industrial sites. The redevelopment of the downtown areas of our cities has allowed the creation of open space where none existed in the past. Occasionally a recreation space is developed on the top of a parking garage. Multi-purpose parks are being created in conjunction with storm retention basins where recharge of underground aquifers has become important. Some have been funded by taxes while others were privately financed.

In some areas recreation space is being provided in subdivisions and housing projects by the developer who uses it as a sales feature. The amount of recreation space is dependent upon the size of the development and the facilities provided relate to the age group to which the project is marketed. Condominiums for retirees rarely have a playground, but a subdivision for young families may have one or more. A large project might include a swimming pool complex, picnic areas, tennis and volleyball courts, racketball, and a clubhouse. When the project is completed these facilities are turned over to a homeowner's association for continued management and maintenance.

Over the decades the design of parks has changed as the needs and desires of people change. Recent emphasis on physical fitness has influenced park design. Playground design has been affected by new materials and the liability problem. This book does not include the principles of park design and recreation planning. Some references have been included at the end of the book for those interested in theory and principles.

To my many colleagues who contributed projects for use in this book, I owe a special debt of gratitude. Without their help this book would not have been possible.

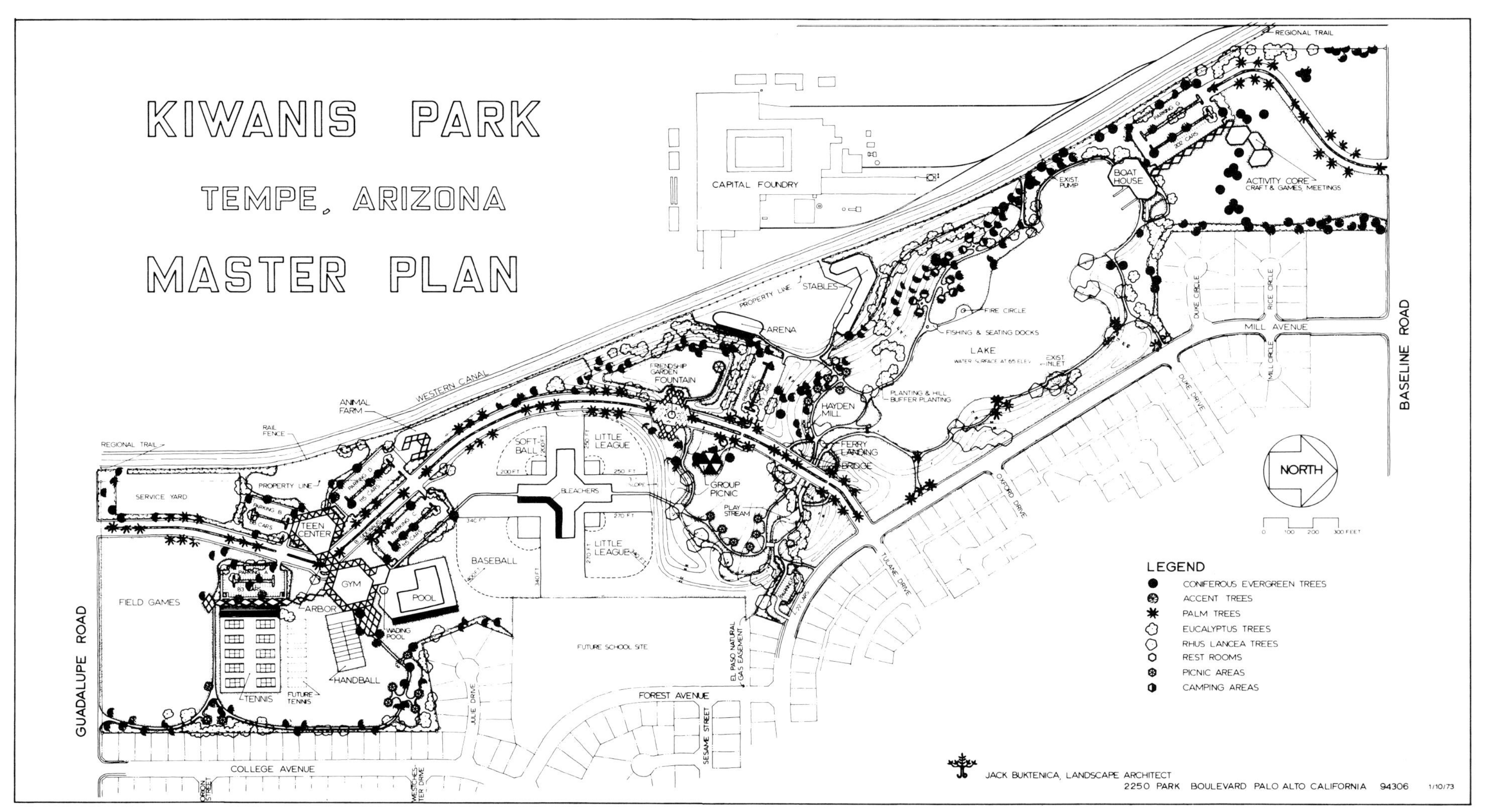

KIWANIS PARK
TEMPE, ARIZONA
MASTER PLAN
REGIONAL TRAIL
CAPITAL FOUNDRY
BASELINE ROAD
EXIST PUMP
BOAT HOUSE
ACTIVITY CORE
CRAFT & GAMES MEETINGS
DUKE CIRCLE
RICE CIRCLE
MILL CIRCLE
MILL AVENUE
STABLES
PROPERTY LINE
FIRE CIRCLE
FISHING & SEATING DOCKS
ARENA
LAKE
WATER SURFACE AT 65 ELEV.
EXIST INLET
FRIENDSHIP GARDEN FOUNTAIN
PLANTING & HILL BUFFER PLANTING
WESTERN CANAL
HAYDEN MILL
DUKE DRIVE
ANIMAL FARM
RAIL FENCE
FERRY LANDING
BRIDGE
REGIONAL TRAIL
PROPERTY LINE
SOFT-BALL
LITTLE LEAGUE
GROUP PICNIC
OXFORD DRIVE
SERVICE YARD
BLEACHERS
PLAY STREAM
NORTH
TEEN CENTER
BASEBALL
LITTLE LEAGUE
GYM
POOL
FIELD GAMES
ARBOR
WADING POOL
FUTURE SCHOOL SITE
EL PASO NATURAL GAS EASEMENT
TULANE DRIVE
0 100 200 300 FEET
HANDBALL
TENNIS
FUTURE TENNIS
JULIE DRIVE
FOREST AVENUE
SESAME STREET
GUADALUPE ROAD
COLLEGE AVENUE
WESTCHES-TER DRIVE
ORION STREET
LEGEND
CONIFEROUS EVERGREEN TREES
ACCENT TREES
PALM TREES
EUCALYPTUS TREES
RHUS LANCEA TREES
REST ROOMS
PICNIC AREAS
CAMPING AREAS
JACK BUKTENICA, LANDSCAPE ARCHITECT
2250 PARK BOULEVARD PALO ALTO CALIFORNIA 94306
1/10/73

KIWANIS PARK

Tempe, Arizona

Design firm: Jack Buktenica Associates

Kiwanis Park is a 127 acre community park, narrow and 1 mile long. It acts as a buffer between residential areas on the east and a foundry on the west. The original site was flat agricultural fields and 300,000 cubic yards of soil was moved to create topographic interest and mounding that will separate park activities from the residential neighborhood. A 20 acre lake collects stormwater runoff in addition to serving several recreational activities. The water level of the lake is 8 feet below the existing curb and sidewalk. With the mounding there is a total elevation change of 30 feet. The higher elevations provide a view of the town and valley.

The park has a historical theme based upon local history. A play stream that flows into the lake is symbolic of the Salt River which borders the north side of the city of Tempe. A bridge over the play stream resembles the first trestle bridge to cross the Salt River several decades ago. The Ferry Boat Landing play structure in the stream is a copy of the original ferry boat that crossed the Salt River at Haydens Landing before any bridges had been built. The Haydens Mill play structure is an abstract version of the original Haydens Mill which was water driven. The town of Tempe was founded by the family of Senator Haydens.

A victorian boat house was designed that reflects the victorian architecture of the original farm house on the site. This boat house will contain the boating concession, a quality restaurant with meeting rooms, and a public sun deck overlooking the lake.

Other facilities in the park include a 15 tennis court complex, a four diamond "wagon wheel" ballfield complex, soccer fields, gymnasium, teen center, aquatics center, group and individual picnic areas, fishing docks, and a friendship garden for the Sister Cities program.

Lake, picnic ramadas and screening mound at Kiwanis Park.

Concrete retaining walls in a series of terraces with sculpture.

Group picnic area at Kiwanis Park.

Cluster of picnic ramadas.

FERRY LANDING & BRIDGE

KIWANIS PARK — TEMPE, ARIZONA

JACK BUKTENICA   LANDSCAPE ARCHITECT   2250 PARK BOULEVARD   PALO ALTO, CALIFORNIA   94306

Bridge at Kiwanis Park resembling railroad bridge over the Salt River.

Pedestrian bridge over the stream near the lake.

BOAT HOUSE

KIWANIS PARK   TEMPE, ARIZONA

JACK BUKTENICA   LANDSCAPE ARCHITECT   2250 PARK BOULEVARD   PALO ALTO, CALIFORNIA   94306

HAYDEN MILL

KIWANIS PARK   TEMPE, ARIZONA

 JACK BUKTENICA   LANDSCAPE ARCHITECT   2250 PARK BOULEVARD   PALO ALTO, CALIFORNIA 94306

GYM & TEEN CENTER ARBOR

KIWANIS PARK   TEMPE, ARIZONA

JACK BUKTENICA   LANDSCAPE ARCHITECT   2250 PARK BOULEVARD   PALO ALTO, CALIFORNIA   94306

GAS WORKS PARK
Seattle, Washington

Design firm: Richard Haag & Associates

A park which is a unique conversion from an industrial site, originally a plant for gas production with its beginnings in 1906. At first coal gas was produced until 1937 when the plant was converted to produce gas from crude oil. Production ended in the 1950's with the city's conversion to natural gas.

A few years later the idea of a park for the site emerged and the purchase of the land followed. Some adjacent land was also purchased to make a 20.5 acre tract with 1,900 lineal feet of waterfront along Lake Union.

The design firm prepared a master plan after a thorough site analysis and proposed to keep a portion of the gas plant for its historic, aesthetic and utilitarian value. This proposal created considerable controversy as the public perception of the plant was that of an object that was ugly and should be demolished. Through an extensive public education program the firm was able to get its proposal accepted. Comparisons were made between the plant's towers and structures with many pieces of contemporary sculpture worldwide which had already been accepted as works of art. Some of the existing buildings and equipment could easily be converted into picnic shelters and play areas.

One of the major problems facing the design firm was the soil which was polluted by chemical wastes from the plant over its approximately 50 years of production. Conventional arboretum type park plantings were not possible. In 1984 the park was closed for testing of hazardous wastes which proved negative and the park was reopened in 1985.

The first phase included the conversion of the boiler house into a picnic shelter, the exhauster house into a children's play barn, and improvement of soil conditions sufficient to allow simple landscaping, mostly grass. The Great Mound was also created at this time. At the completion of this phase in 1975, the park was opened to the public.

Phase two included the development of the southeast parking area, the concrete prow, pathways along the water, and pruning of plant tower appendages which might encourage climbing.

In the third phase the following were added: additional play equipment, park furniture, an esplanade along the water, and a monumental sundial on the Great Mound.

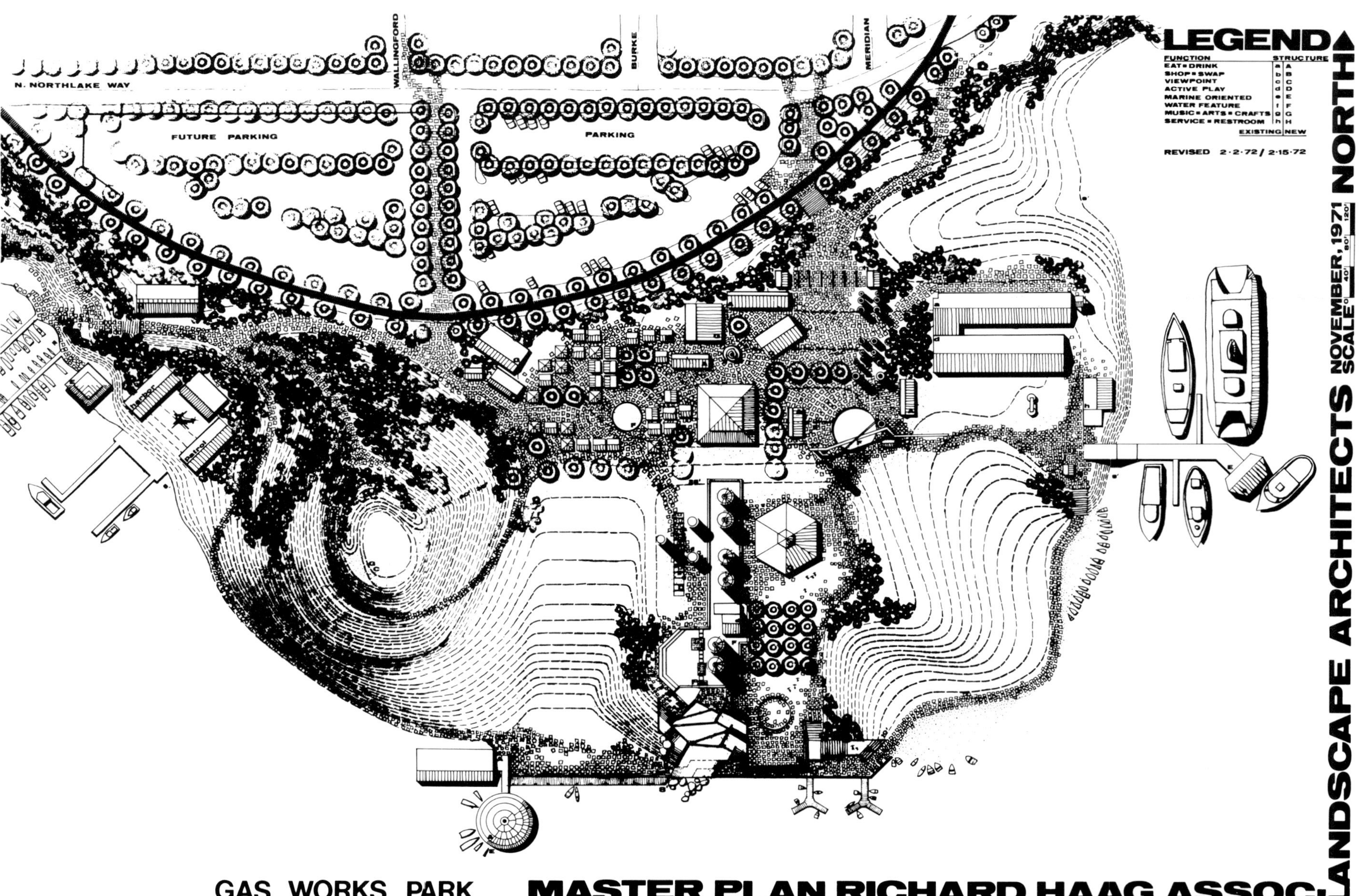

LEGEND
NORTH►
FUNCTION
EAT • DRINK
SHOP • SWAP
VIEWPOINT
ACTIVE PLAY
MARINE ORIENTED
WATER FEATURE
MUSIC • ARTS • CRAFTS
SERVICE • RESTROOM
STRUCTURE
a A
b B
c C
d D
e E
f F
g G
h H
EXISTING NEW
REVISED 2·2·72 / 2·15·72
N. NORTHLAKE WAY
FUTURE PARKING
PARKING
WALLINGFORD
BURKE
MERIDIAN
LANDSCAPE ARCHITECTS NOVEMBER, 1971 SCALE 40' 80' 120'
GAS WORKS PARK MASTER PLAN RICHARD HAAG ASSOC-

Gas Works Park as viewed from the Great Mound which is on the west side of the park.

Structures which cover some of the painted piping and equipment. On the left is the restroom and concession building.

Play area with some conventional equipment on the south side of the structures.

Refurbished gas plant equipment used for play.

GRASSLAWN PARK
Redmond, Washington

Design firm: Jongejan/Gerrard/McNeal

Grasslawn is a large 32-acre multi-use park. It is located in a residential area along a major arterial where it has been the center of community activity since its completion.

Facilities include three softball fields (two lighted) with spectator areas, six tennis courts (three lighted), an all-weather soccer field (also lighted) and outdoor basketball courts. In addition, two areas have play equipment for less structured activities.

There is also a jogging trail, a fitness course, picnic tables and game tables. A large meadow is used for picnics and informal games, and a domed shelter is available for group picnics. A building provides restrooms and a service/maintenance area.

Although much of Grasslawn Park is designed for organized and structured play, about a third of the site has been left in an almost wild state. Early in the planning of the park community residents requested the retention of the wooded areas of the site. A small parking area serves this part of the park while a larger one is located near the athletic fields.

Much of the site was wet and boggy most of the year requiring the installation of an extensive sub-surface drainage system before the athletic fields could be built. Earth forms (or mounds) were used to separate activity areas and contour the flat site thus permitting simultaneous activities to occur.

Because the park is in a residential neighborhood, lighted fields were grouped in an area where they could be screened as much as possible. Rows of trees were planted to screen lighted courts from neighbors and also to divide fields within the park. To reinforce the park-like aspects of the site and to blend with its surroundings, wood and wire-mesh fencing was used throughout.

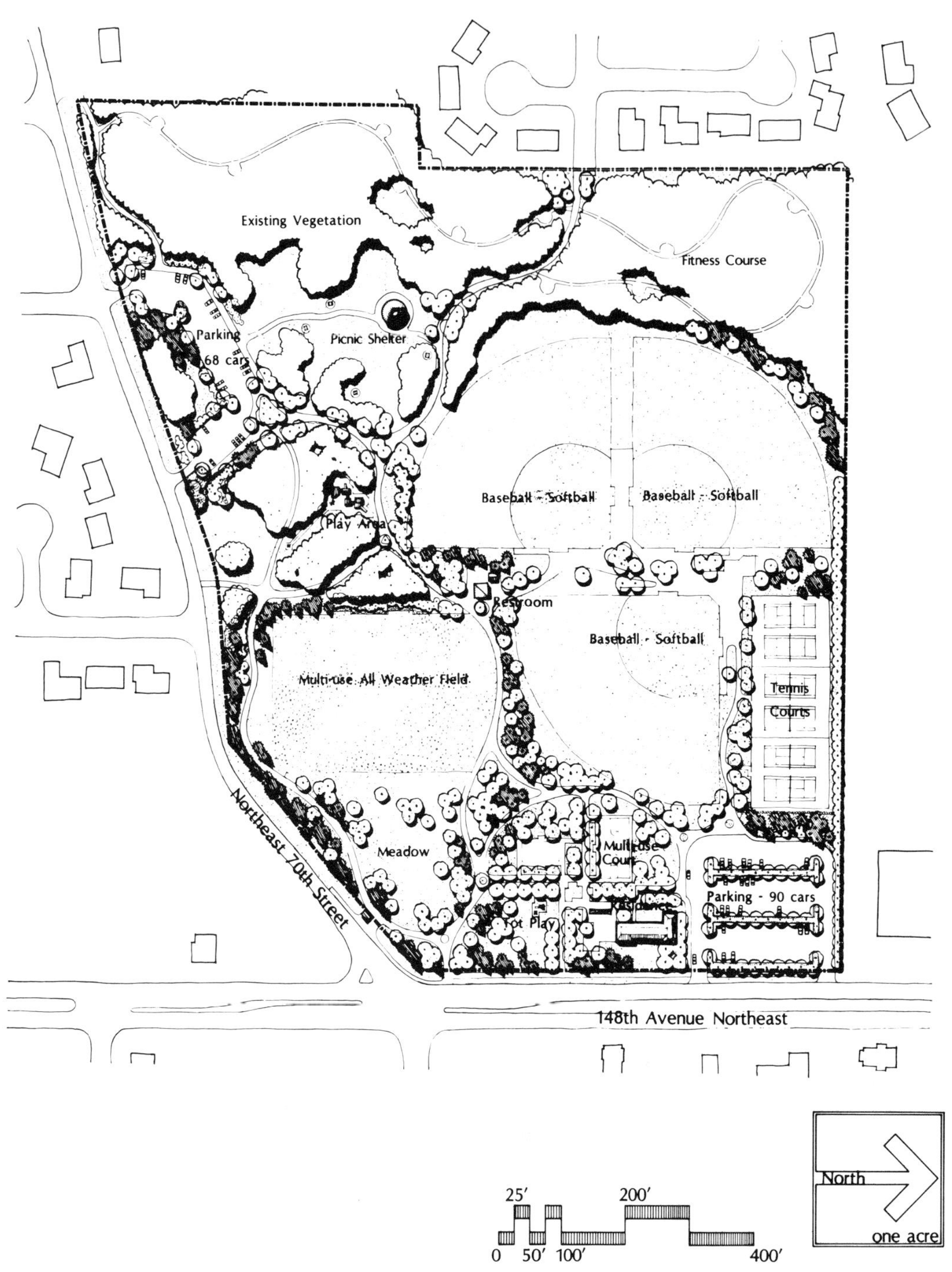

Grass Lawn Park

Redmond Department of Parks and Recreation

Softball field with timber fence.

Tennis courts with timber fence.

Basketball court with screen mounding.

Restrooms and service equipment storage and supplies.

Timber play structure in a wooded environment.

Picnic shelter at Grass Lawn Park.

Terraced parking lot with planted islands at Grass Lawn Park.

LUTHER BURBANK PARK
Mercer Island, Washington

Design firm: Jongejan/Gerrard/McNeal

On an island close to Seattle, this 72 acre park provides the only open space left on the island which is heavily urbanized. Most of the facilities are clustered to retain the open space. These include tennis courts, play area, and amphitheater all adjacent to a large parking lot. The remainder of the park offers solitude to walkers, joggers, bicyclists and bird-watchers.

The play area features upright concrete forms which serve as climbing structures, anchors for swinging bridges made of wood and rope, and one hollow tower doubles as a playhouse fort and climbing place. A concrete ramp leads to a cable ride, a popular play element. All of the structures and rides encourage adult participation.

The amphitheater is a series of grass terraces sculptured into the hillside with the stage area defined by wooden baffles. In good weather it is used for plays, dance performances and concerts by both amateur and professional groups.

Because much of the park is low-bank shoreline adjacent to a deep channel in the lake, there is quality fishing available. There is also a swimming beach and boat dock.

Play area.

Brick pyramids in play area at Burbank Park.

Additional views of play area.

Steel and glass picnic shelter.

Terraced seating areas for tennis court on the right.

Amphitheatre with grass terraces and timber retaining walls.

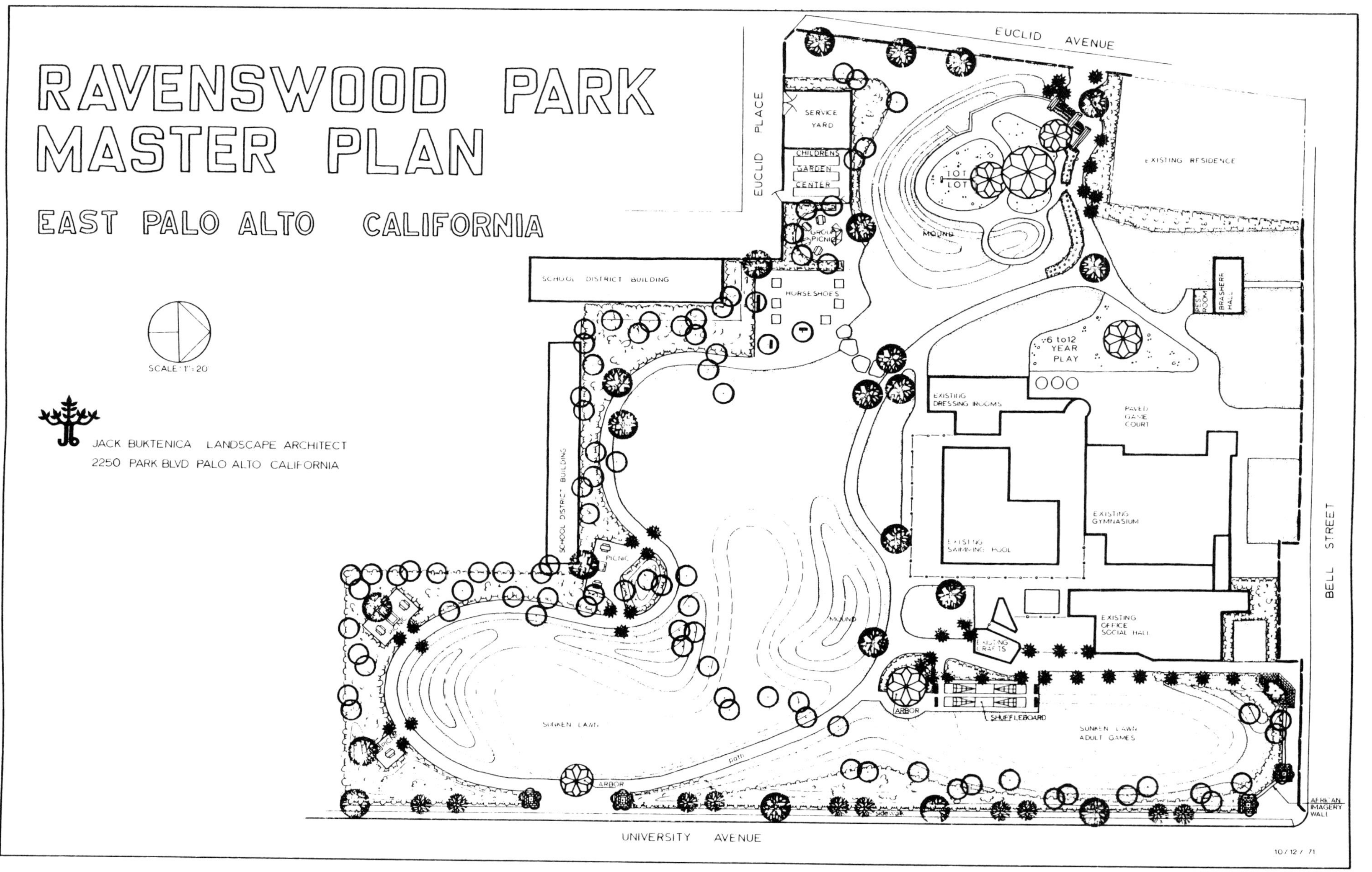

RAVENSWOOD PARK
MASTER PLAN
EAST PALO ALTO CALIFORNIA
SCALE 1"=20'
JACK BUKTENICA LANDSCAPE ARCHITECT
2250 PARK BLVD PALO ALTO CALIFORNIA
EUCLID PLACE
EUCLID AVENUE
SERVICE YARD
CHILDRENS GARDEN CENTER
GROUP PICNIC
SCHOOL DISTRICT BUILDING
HORSESHOES
LOT LOT
MOUND
EXISTING RESIDENCE
PRESS ROOM
BRASHER HALL
6 to12 YEAR PLAY
EXISTING DRESSING ROOMS
PAVED GAME COURT
EXISTING GYMNASIUM
EXISTING SWIMMING POOL
EXISTING OFFICE SOCIAL HALL
BELL STREET
SCHOOL DISTRICT BUILDING
PICNIC
MOUND
EXISTING RAFTS
ARBOR
SHUFFLEBOARD
SUNKEN LAWN
ARBOR
PATH
SUNKEN LAWN ADULT GAMES
AFRICAN IMAGERY WALL
UNIVERSITY AVENUE
10/12/71

RAVENSWOOD PARK
East Palo Alto, California

Design firm: Jack Buktenica Associates

Ravenswood Park is a 5-acre site and the design reflects an African theme assigned by the recreation district in harmony with the historical background of the community. The native African hut, African animals, and African plant materials were used as the dominant imagery to establish the theme. Three "hut-kiosks" were grouped together in the pre-school play area to form an intimate sense of space that shelters the play apparatus. One kiosk contains a bird cage or mini-aviary. A 9-foot tall wooden giraffe serves as a support for the tot swings. Other African animals are cast in a concrete wall that also serves to enclose the space.

The "hut-kiosk" as a single unit repeats itself at the senior citizen area and houses built-in tables with checker boards in the tile tops. A shuffle board is located close by. The kiosk is repeated again at the park entrance with seating.

The temperate climate at this site allowed the use of many native African plants.

Picnic kiosk with African theme.

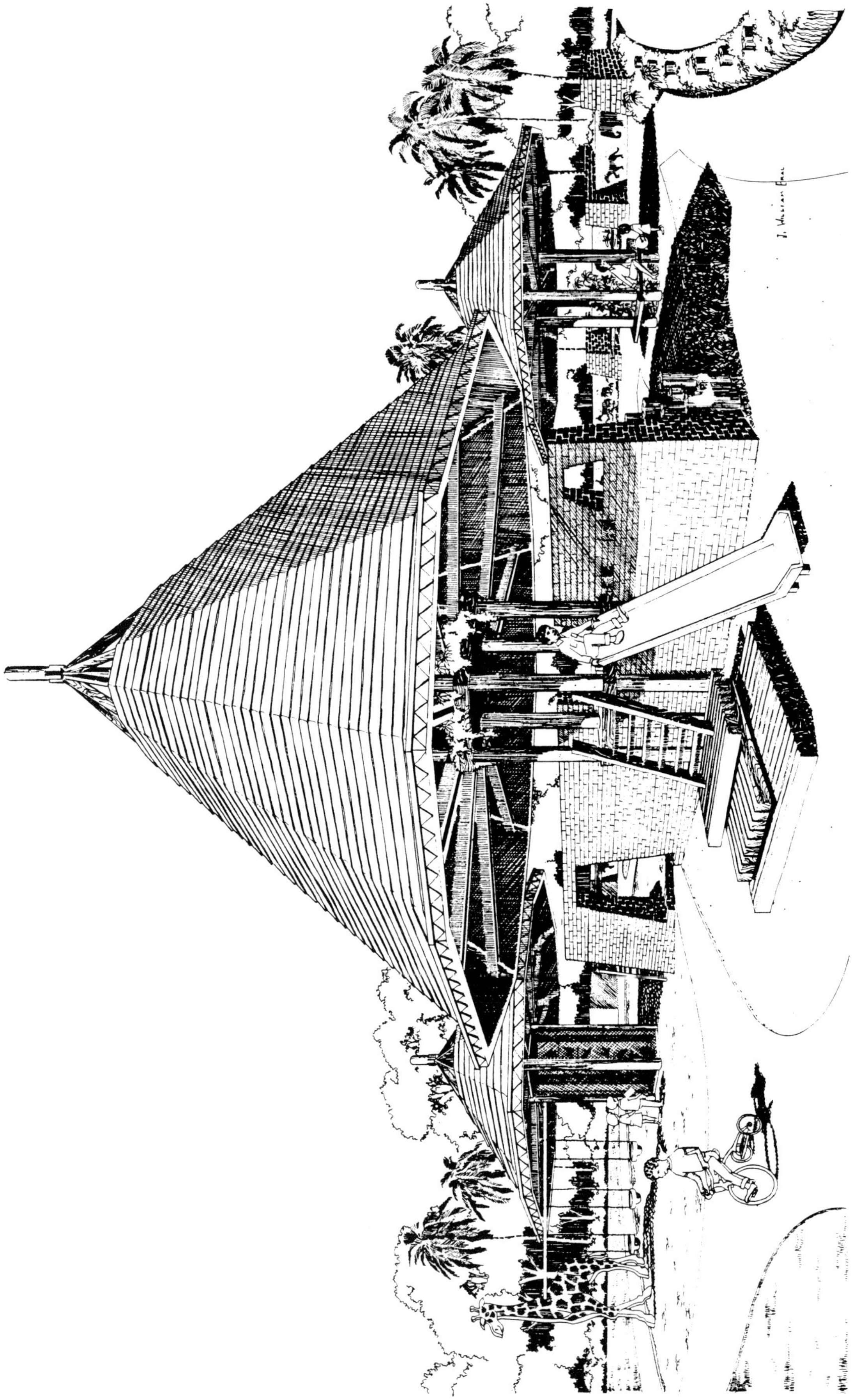

RAVENSWOOD PARK

Kiosk sheltered play area with giraffe support for swings.

Play area under kiosk structure at Ravenswood Park.

Two additional views of Ravenswood Park.

TIMKEN MINI-PARK
Canton, Ohio

Design firm: Bonnell & Associates

Developed from a gravel parking lot, this park was created to improve the physical appearance of the company offices and factory environment as well as provide a pleasant outdoor noon time and after hour meeting place for employees. New trees, shrubs, benches, tables, lights and accent paving were used. The appearance of the surrounding buildings was also improved to enhance the total environment adjacent to the park.

Lunch time seating areas for employees.

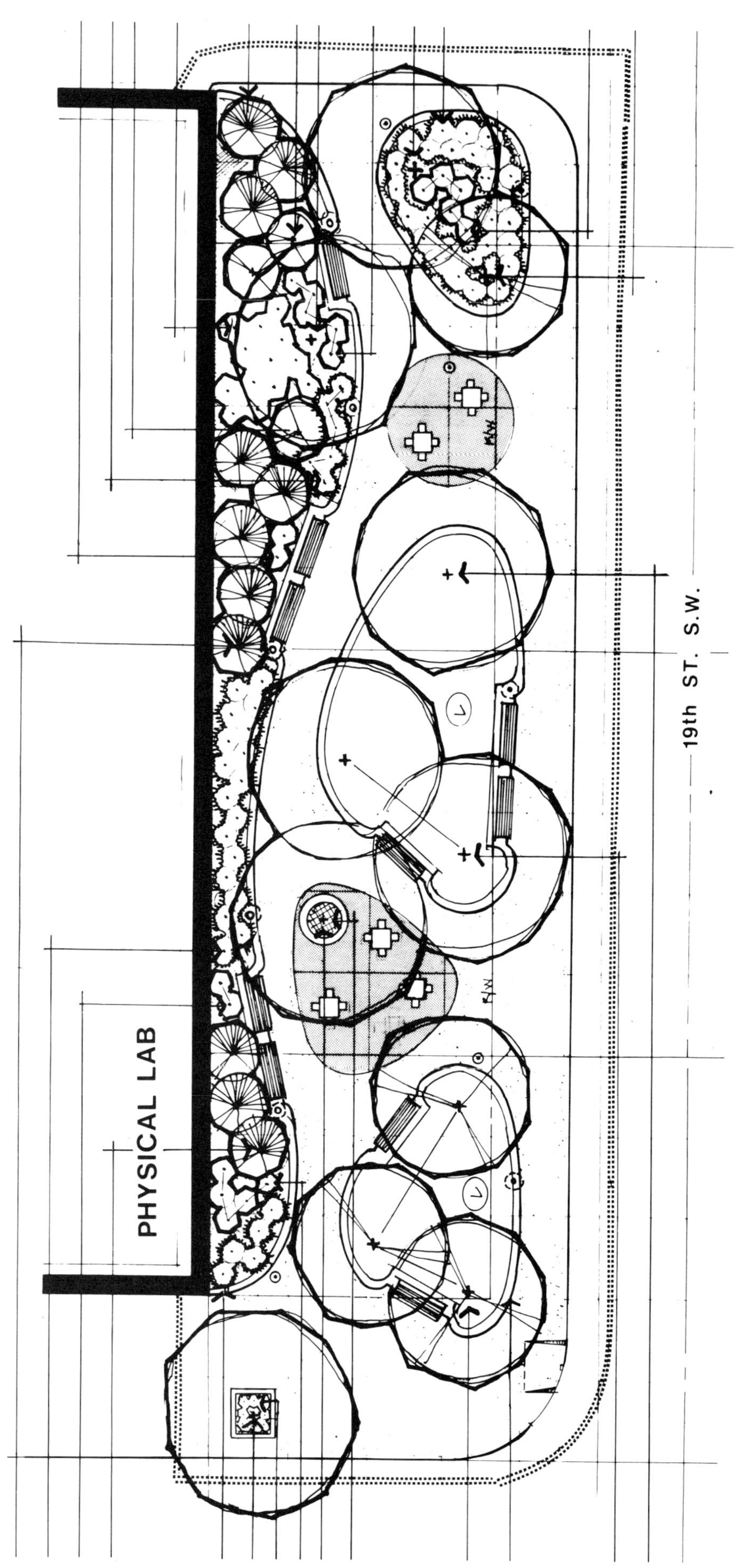

Master Plan for Timken Mini-Park.

Parking lot before it was converted to a park.

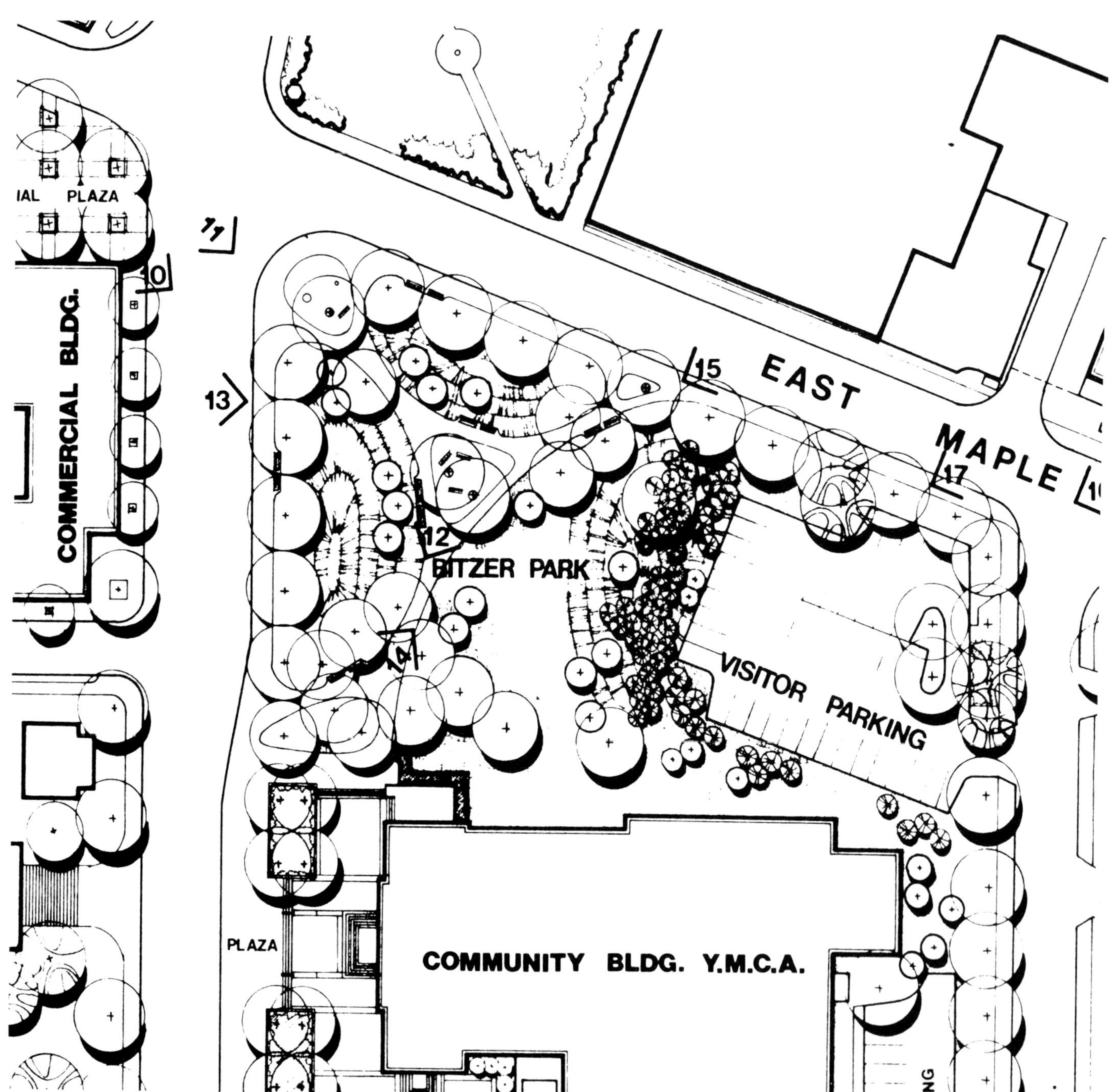

Master Plan for Bitzer Park.

BITZER PARK
North Canton, Ohio

Design firm: Bonnell & Associates

This park was created as part of a renewal effort in downtown North Canton. The downtown area had declined with the rapid growth of the city and the movement of businesses to outlying shopping centers. Federal funds were not used in this renewal effort but the park was financed by concerned property owners and the Hoover Foundation (the Hoover Company is a major local employer).

The design provided a major addition of green space for the downtown area. Curvilinear sidewalks with benches, lighting, mounding and trees make up the bulk of the design.

Entry to Bitzer Park. Photo by Don Teal.

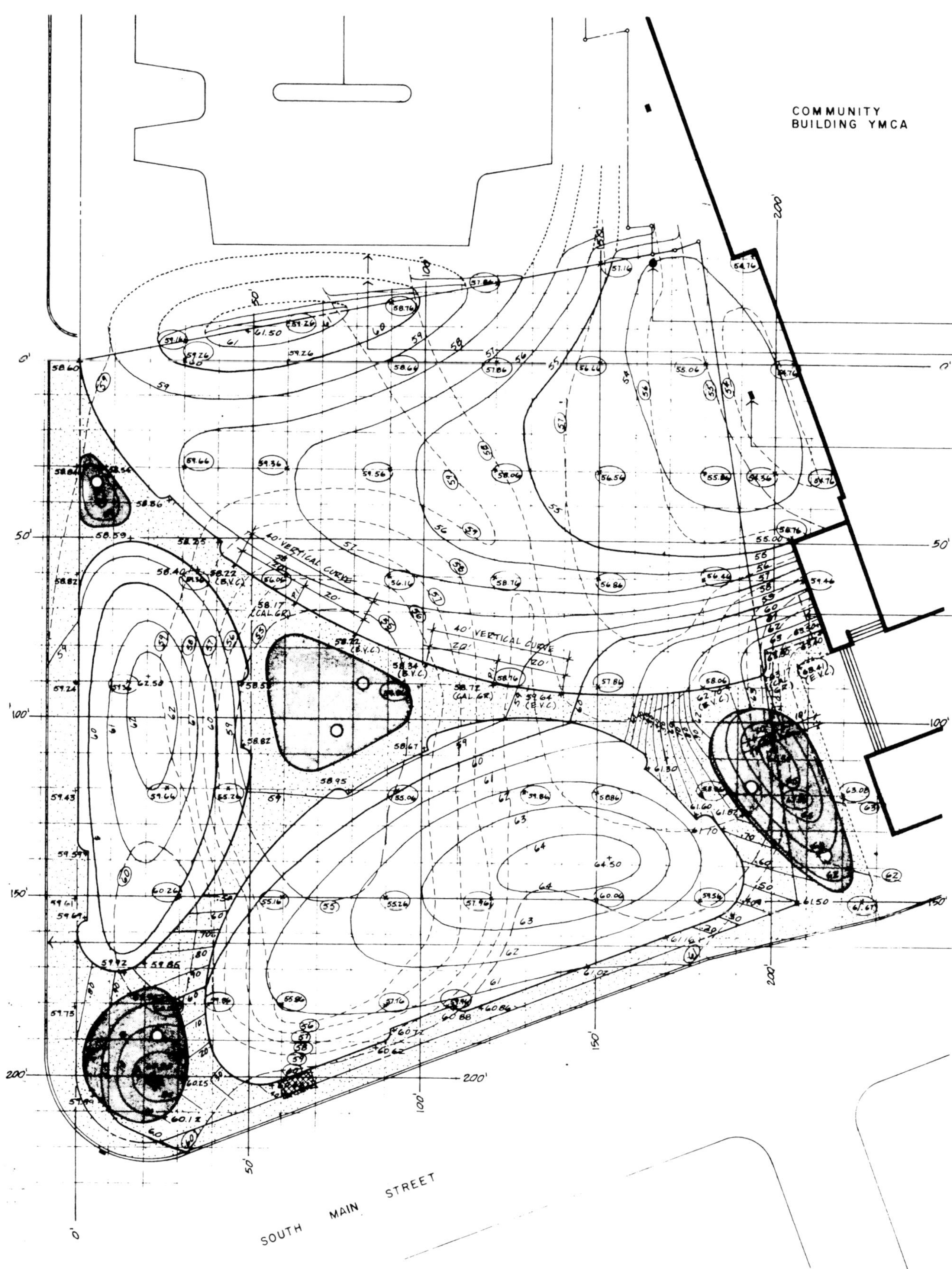

Plan for the mounding of Bitzer Park.

Walk through Bitzer Park with seating, mounding and planting. Photo by Don Teal.

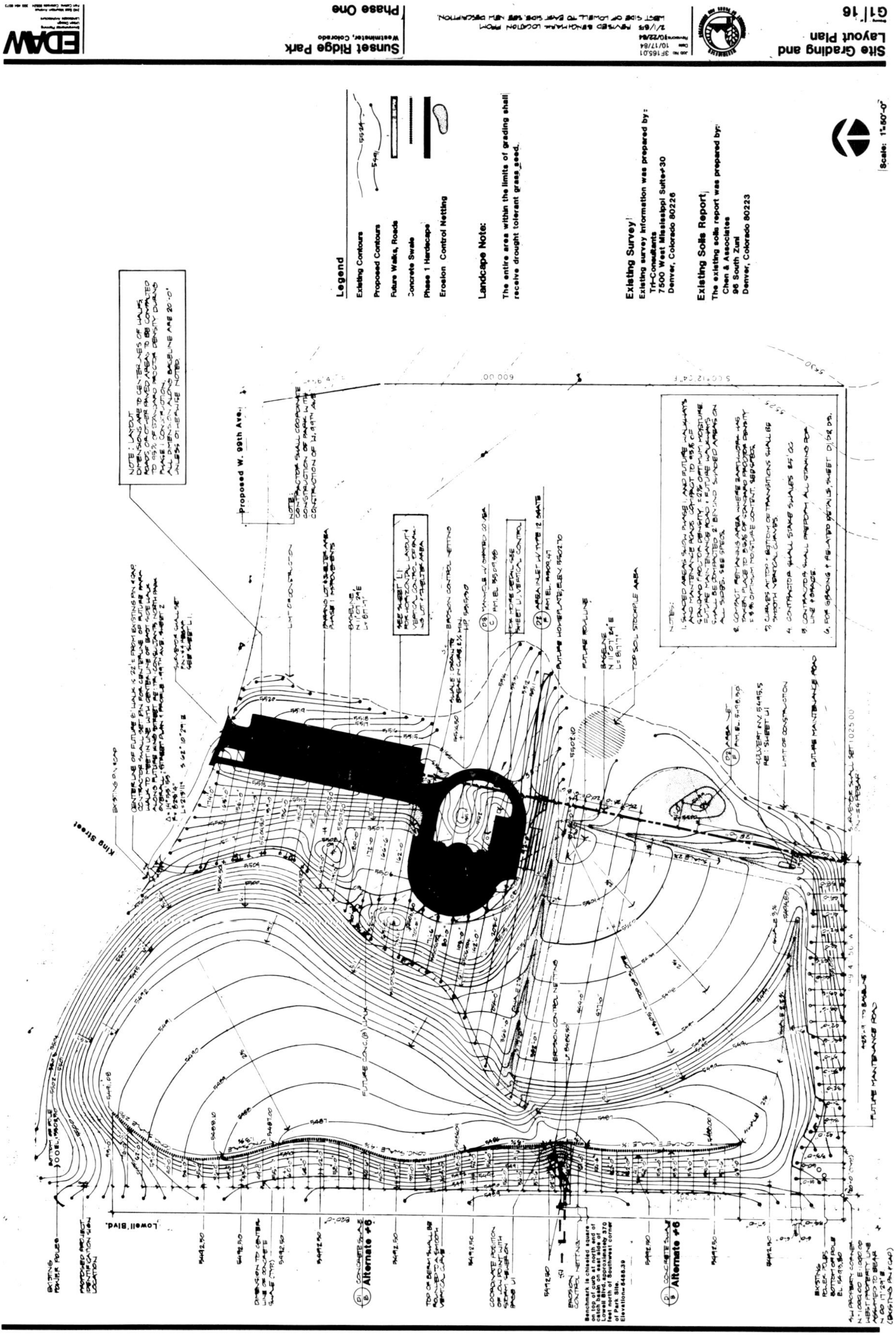

Site and grading plan for Sunset Ridge Park.

SUNSET RIDGE PARK
Westminster, Colorado

Design firm: EDAW, Inc.

A 21-acre site for both a park and elementary school. The master plan includes a 4-acre elementary school site, a football/soccer field, a softball field, picnic shelter, restroom, playground, basketball court, parking lot, landscaped areas, and an 11 acre-foot storm water detention pond. The master plan was developed through input from neighbors, homeowner associations, and developers.

Play tube apparatus.

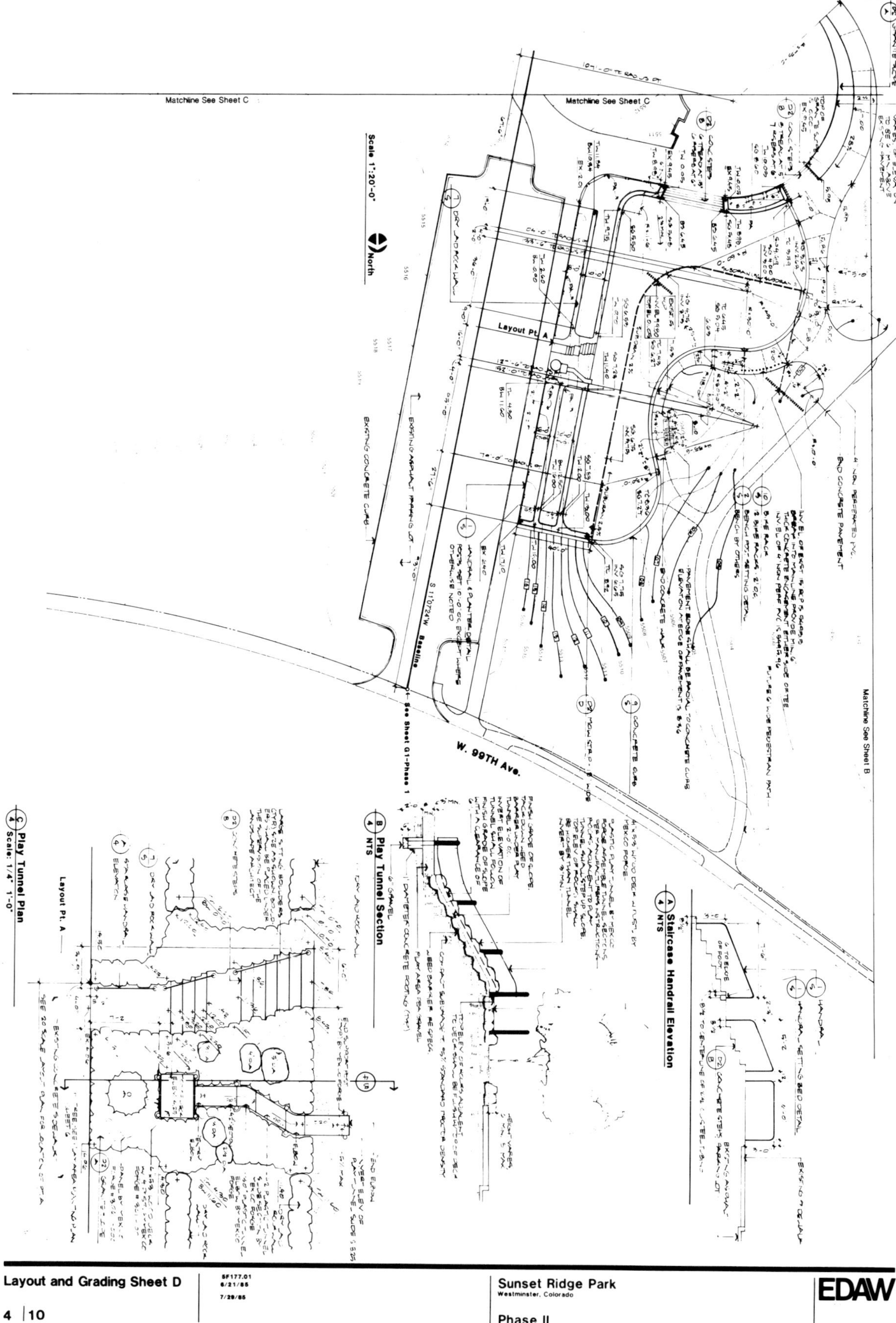

Layout and Grading Sheet D

SF177.01
6/21/85
7/29/85

4 | 10

Sunset Ridge Park
Westminster, Colorado

Phase II

EDAW

Picnic shelter and volleyball court.

Play area, volleyball court and shelter at Sunset Ridge Park.

Play area at Sunset Ridge Park.

TOMMY PERKINS MEMORIAL PARK
Olney, Texas

Design firm: Myrick Newman Dahlberg & Partners

When designing this park, the desire of the client, Mr. and Mrs. Tommy Perkins, was to create a symbolic memorial where veterans and the families of those killed in war could be honored and comforted. The park was to be a place of recreation and relaxation that also stood for the American way.

The major obstacle which later became the catalyst for design was the size and status of the City of Olney. How is one to design a symbolic park within a small, West Texas oil community without offending neighbors or creating a project that stands alone?

The designers drew from the City's existing architecture including farm homes, simple overhanging structures and metal buildings to design a blue, tubular steel framed memorial with aluminum roofing. The structures are placed among an existing grove of pecan trees whose gnarled character contrasts with the simplicity of the architectural elements.

Within the memorial pavillion, a simple monument of black Brazilian granite is inscribed with text by the main donor for the park. Other contributions and guidance from the community leaders were developed through a series of design sessions directed under the guidance of the landscape architect.

The park is a bold, yet conservative, statement in a small conservative community which epitomizes the strong feeling of patriotism and commitment to American ideals.

Scale model of park.

Park structures in pecan grove.

SUDDIETH PARK
Akron, Ohio

Design firm: Bonnell & Associates

Three-quarters of an acre in size, this mini-park is on the north side of Akron. The design represents a renovation of an existing park with drainage problems and few facilities.

With citizen input the designers prepared a master plan which incorporated a need for separating age groups and their activities, eliminating wet areas, developing more stimulating play experiences and providing barriers to auto traffic.

A buffer was provided to separate the older children using the basketball court from the small children using the play area. The play area was built into an existing slope to reinforce this separation. A combination storage building and play structure was designed with a ladder to the upper deck, slide and fireman's pole. Other play amenities were added as well as benches and bollards to separate the play area from the adjacent road.

Entrance area to park with play structures in the background.

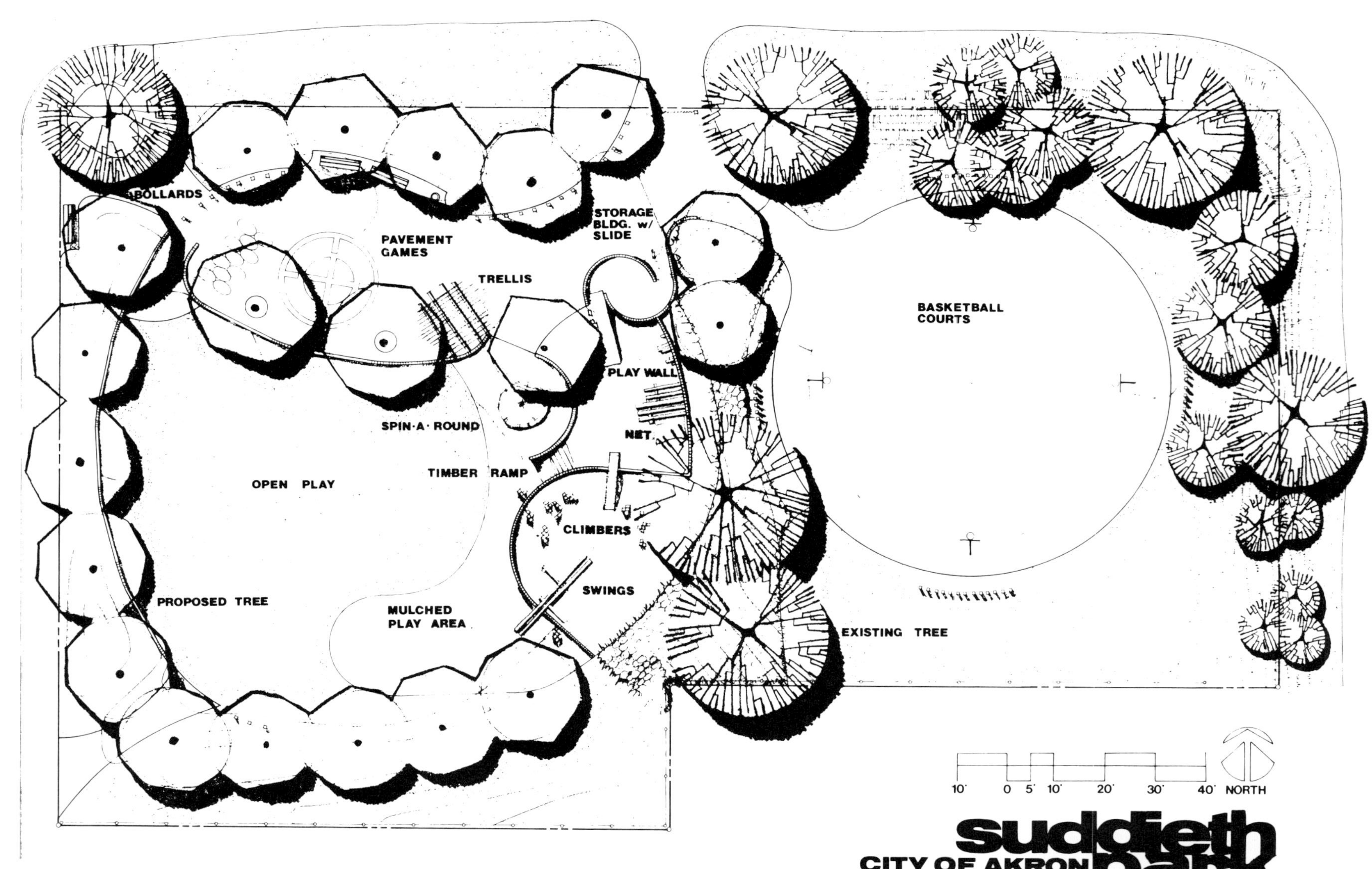

CARPENTER STREET
MILDRED AVENUE
BOLLARDS
PAVEMENT GAMES
TRELLIS
STORAGE BLDG. w/ SLIDE
SPIN·A·ROUND
PLAY WALL
NET
OPEN PLAY
TIMBER RAMP
CLIMBERS
PROPOSED TREE
MULCHED PLAY AREA
SWINGS
EXISTING TREE
BASKETBALL COURTS
10 0 5 10 20 30 40 NORTH
sudfeth park
CITY OF AKRON OHIO
MASTER PLAN DEVELOPMENT

mildred street
bus stop
court games
trellis
access
play/storage structure
buffer
open play area
multi-level play area
basketball courts
salome avenue
suddeth park

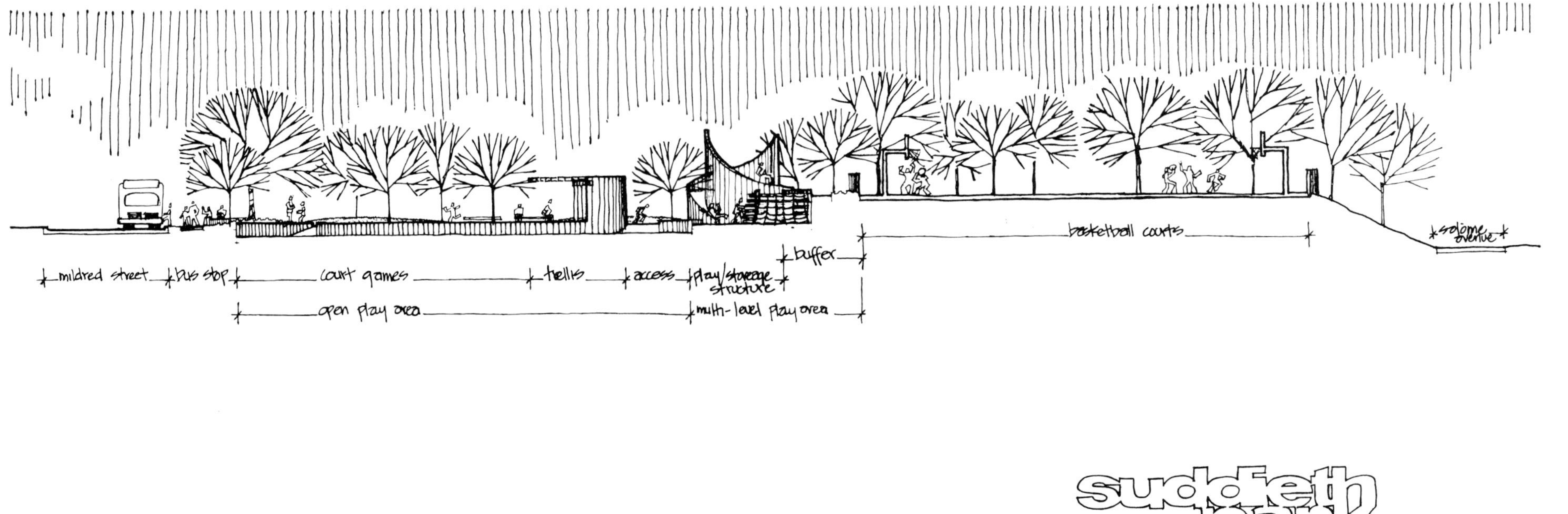

47

Timber play structures.

Timber play structures at Suddieth Park.

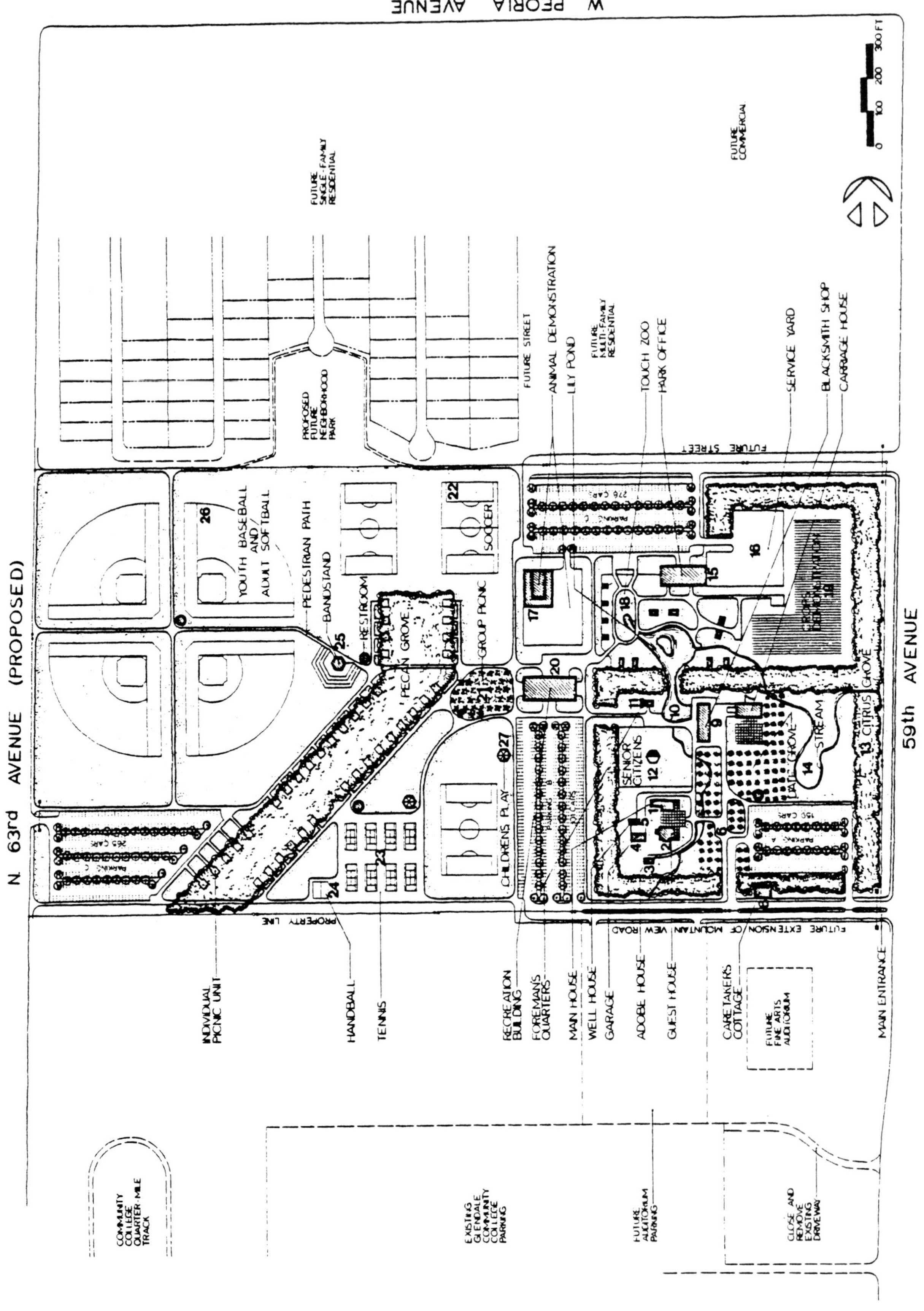

Master plan for Sahuaro Ranch Park.

SAHUARO RANCH PARK
Glendale, Arizona

Design firm: Jack Buktenica Associates

This park is an 80 acre site, half of which is a historical restoration of an early ranch, and half is developed for general recreation.

The vegetative patterns at the ranch included agricultural groves of citrus, olives, dates and pecans. Ornamental patterns included an Ash tree tunnel that flanked the original entrance and fan palms that lined paths and driveways. The groves of fruiting trees were saved where possible, and replaced or added to as necessary. By the time of development many of the Ash trees were declining or dead. They were used again along the new park entrance which is the same alignment as the original ranch entrance. New paths in the park were lined with fan palms to maintain the original vegetative pattern.

The original stucco entrance piers were moved to a pedestrian entrance. New piers of the same design, but larger in scale were installed for the main entrance to receive the gates, entry arch, and security fence.

In the early days of the Ranch (late 1800s), there was a peacock crossing at the entrance to the ranch which was identified with a sign. Town folk reportedly came out in the early evening to watch the peacocks cross 59th Avenue. Peacocks still live on the ranch site in the shelter of the citrus groves. The 10 foot diameter steel peacock at the park entrance is an expression of this history and serves as the park logo. The wrought iron entrance arch is a stylistic detail that was popular in the period which the ranch was developed. The entrance piers and wrought iron detail repeat at the children's play and group picnic areas.

Cast iron light posts with period fixtures are used along the main entrance, the parking lots, and the park paths as an expression of the historical period of the ranch.

The historic pecan grove is the setting for many individual picnic sites with barbecues. The major playfields of soccer and baseball are recessed to clearly define the space and provide slopes for spectator seating on the grass.

The following is a statement of philosophy by the designer which he has titled, PLAYGROUNDS THAT INVITE CELEBRATION:

Celebration is joyous formal acknowledgment of an experience. We set the stage for celebration in theatre, organized sports, religious worship, and other activities. After the commitment or decision to play, the key element to setting the stage for celebration is a sense of arrival. The total play area needs to read as a very special space honoring the apparatus and activities within. The apparatus and activities become part of a series of complimentary spaces that flow together to form the playground. This requires the use of structural or architectural elements, shaping or contouring the land (both depressing and mounding), and intimate spaces for observing and resting. Properly executed, the architecture becomes a landmark symbol that stimulates excitement about arrival upon approaching.

At Sahuaro Ranch the landmark symbol is an extension of the theme architecture at the main entrance to the park which makes the space more "total site specific." The symbol serves as a draw for the passive as well as active participant thus promoting use for all ages. This symbol at the play area is the bridge with an arbor detailed similarly to the main park entrance. The arbor helps to create intimate seating areas that overlook the play area. This type of seating for older persons enable them to share in the joy of play and perhaps recall past experience. The space under the bridge provides a tunnel connecting two sides of the playground and has integrated seats for playground participants. Custom and manufactured play apparatus is set up in individual spaces for each activity. This is accomplished by use of play walls, trees, and creating depressed and mounded areas. Small scale picnic tables are introduced for children to create their special picnic experience. Full scale picnic tables are also included to encourage the entire family to share the experience. The entire space is defined by either a perimeter walk or depression or mound. Where applicable the area could be further secured with a complete wrought iron fence with controlled access.

The thoughtful balance of activities combined with the thoughtful definition of the total playground space can accommodate physical release of tensions as well as passive niches to rest and calm the mind.

Texture and finishes on equipment and all improvements are important considerations to encourage intimate contact with all elements. A balance in color range from bright to pastel is more appealing than an abundance of harsh bright or all dull pastel.

Plant materials in the form of grass and trees are primary. This should be a reprieve from the heat and asphalt jungle.

Size of equipment relative to particular age groups is important so that equipment is challenging without imposing physical dangers. The element of risk is inherent from birth. Reasonable thought and care in planning playgrounds is mandatory. Elimination of risk is impossible. It is difficult to keep this in perspective with the current liability crisis facing all areas of our community. Creative energy needs to be invested in the areas of liability to guarantee a stimulating environment for play and celebration.

Play area with concrete sculpture.

Play area with slide, bridge-structure combination.

Play area entry structure.

North section of play area.

Designer's concept for the band stand at Sahuaro Ranch Park.

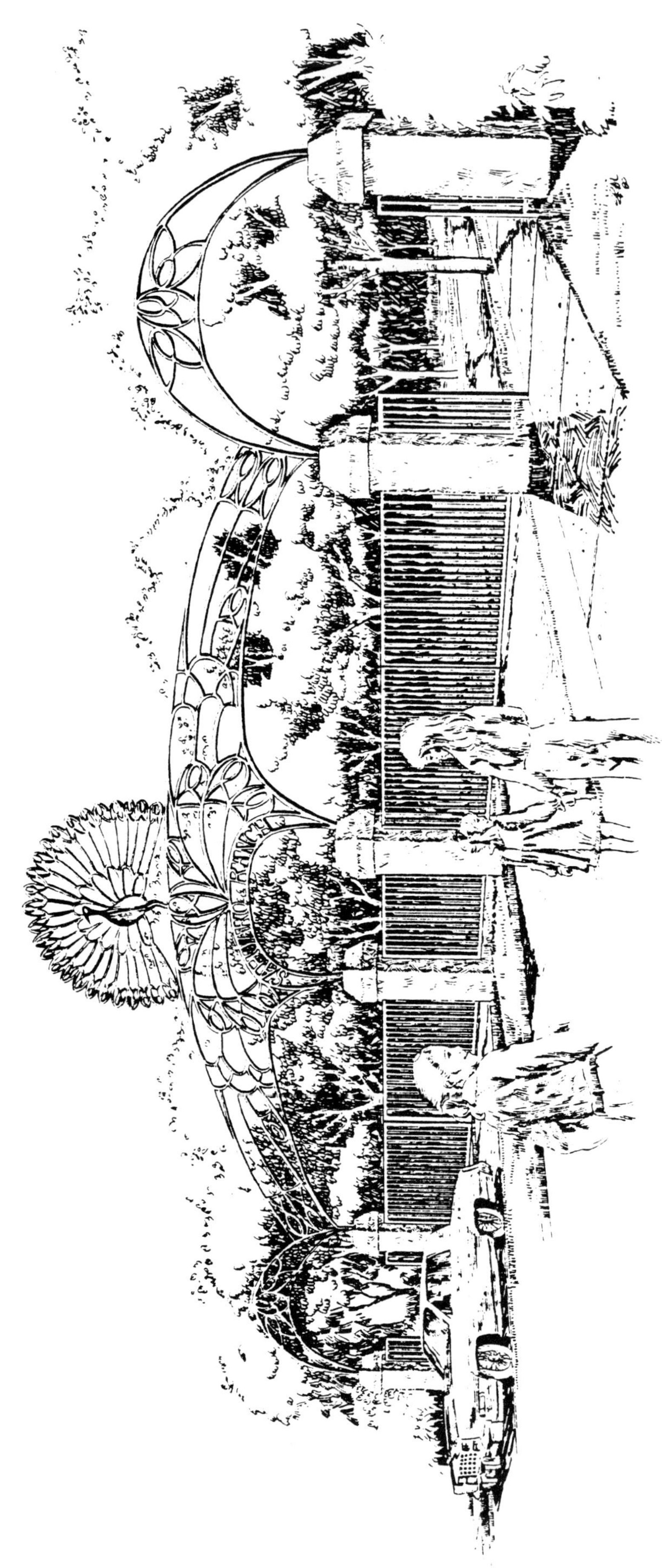

Concept sketch for park entrance.

Park entrance gates and structure.

Group picnic and cooking area at Sahuaro Ranch Park.

Concept sketch for carriage house pavilion.

Historic buildings at Sahuaro Ranch Park.

Scale model for the Highland Park Playground.

HIGHLAND PARK PLAYGROUND
Dallas, Texas

Design firm: Myrick Newman Dahlberg & Partners

This playground serves the day care school program of the United Methodist Church. It was designed for motor skill development and activity levels of pre-school toddlers to six year olds. Facilities include several play structures as well as a diaper changing table, underground "caves" and above grade forts for the enjoyment of the children.

Special "splash days" are organized allowing kids to wade in the sunken amphitheater area, as well as play under special "rain sprays" mounted in vertical wood structures above paved areas. Two small children's restrooms, writing/drawing walls, trickway, swinging bridge, a maze, and rope and tire swings, all add to the variety and play options available to the children.

Six views of the play equipment and structures at Highland Park. See page 64 for two.

EDGAR M. QUEENY PLAY CENTER

St. Louis County, Missouri

Design firm: Sverdrup Corporation

This playground occupies a one-acre site and is designed to serve children of all ages with a special orientation toward those between 3 and 10 years. The design of this facility was based upon in-depth research into children's recreational needs and desires and incorporates a wide variety of creative, physical, and imaginative play activities under County Parks Department supervision and direction. The day center nature of the play area affords parents the opportunity to enjoy the many adult facilities in the remainder of the adjacent park while their children are safely occupied in a supervised play environment.

The site is divided into three areas: (1) active interplay, (2) creative play, and (3) passive recreation. The active interplay area used units of Timberform wood play equipment with a sand base. Along the eastern slope of the playground, a stone mountain structure was designed and built. It offers a variety of play experiences including climbing, sliding, swinging, crawling, and jumping. A tunnel provides a lower level of play which is tied to the upper level by a vertical passage with a ladder.

The creative play area is close to the playground headquarters where children gain creative play experiences through the use of construction toys and arts and crafts.

The passive recreation area consists of the upper slope along the west edge of the playground with immediate shade for adults to sit and observe their children at play below. Sidewalks and steps provide easy access to the playground.

Entrance and overview of the play area.

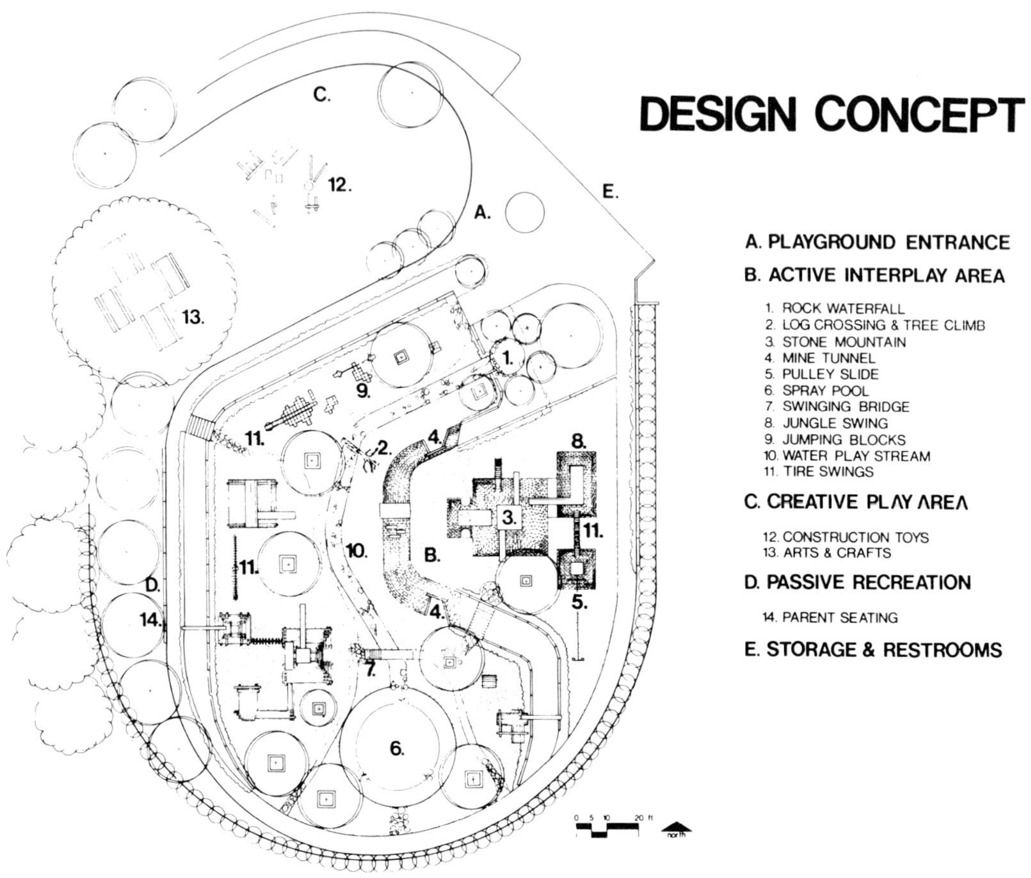

DESIGN CONCEPT

A. PLAYGROUND ENTRANCE

B. ACTIVE INTERPLAY AREA

1. ROCK WATERFALL
2. LOG CROSSING & TREE CLIMB
3. STONE MOUNTAIN
4. MINE TUNNEL
5. PULLEY SLIDE
6. SPRAY POOL
7. SWINGING BRIDGE
8. JUNGLE SWING
9. JUMPING BLOCKS
10. WATER PLAY STREAM
11. TIRE SWINGS

C. CREATIVE PLAY AREA

12. CONSTRUCTION TOYS
13. ARTS & CRAFTS

D. PASSIVE RECREATION

14. PARENT SEATING

E. STORAGE & RESTROOMS

Master plan and concept drawings.

Play equipment and structures.

Closeup views of some of the play equipment and structures at the Queeny Play Center.

One of two totem poles in the park.

Raised areas provide soil depth for grass and trees.

VICTOR STEINBRUECK PARK
Seattle, Washington

Design firm: Richard Haag & Associates

Originally known as Market Park, this 1-acre site is a city open-space extension of the Pike Place Public Market in Seattle's central business district. The park was co-designed by architect Victor Steinbrueck and renamed as a memorial in his honor. The park was designed to be unpretentious and somewhat anonymous in character in order to harmonize with the traditional market setting and spectacular view of Puget Sound and the Olympic Mountains.

The design involved the development of the park over a three level parking garage through an arrangement made between the City and a private company who owns and operates the parking garage. This brought the park to street level on the uphill side. Facilities include picnic tables and shelter, a children's play area, sturdy wooden benches, grassy berms and concrete seat walls for lunching or just sitting and watching.

After completion of the park two 50 foot wooden totem poles were added as a tribute to the cultural contribution and heritage of our Native Americans. They form a belvedere to look out at Puget Sound and the distant Olympic Mountains and frequent colorful sunsets.

Picnic and lounging areas on a garage rooftop.

Play courtyard.

Glass enclosure connecting recreation facilities.

RECREATION CENTER FOR THE HANDICAPPED
Dallas, Texas

Design firms: Myrick Newman Dahlberg & Partners
Parkey and Partners

On a 10 acre wooded site located adjacent to Bachman Lake, the design team created a glass gallery or spine that connects auditorium, gymnasium, natatorium and multi-purpose recreation rooms while forming four exterior court spaces such as two different outdoor class areas, adaptive play space and a multi-use play court. Care was taken to preserve the valuable Post Oak Grove and to nestle the building complex under this living canopy.

The adaptive play area created varying challenges for the handicapped such as a flexible maze play structure made of colorful plexiglass panels that can be removed from a rigid frame to form various tunnels or small rooms, wood climbing devices and forts to test motor skills, slides, and a running water channel for boat floating.

The multi-purpose play court provides basketball, tetherball, shuffleboard, volleyball and badminton activities along with access to Bachman Lake's jogging and bike trail system.

Play courtyard.

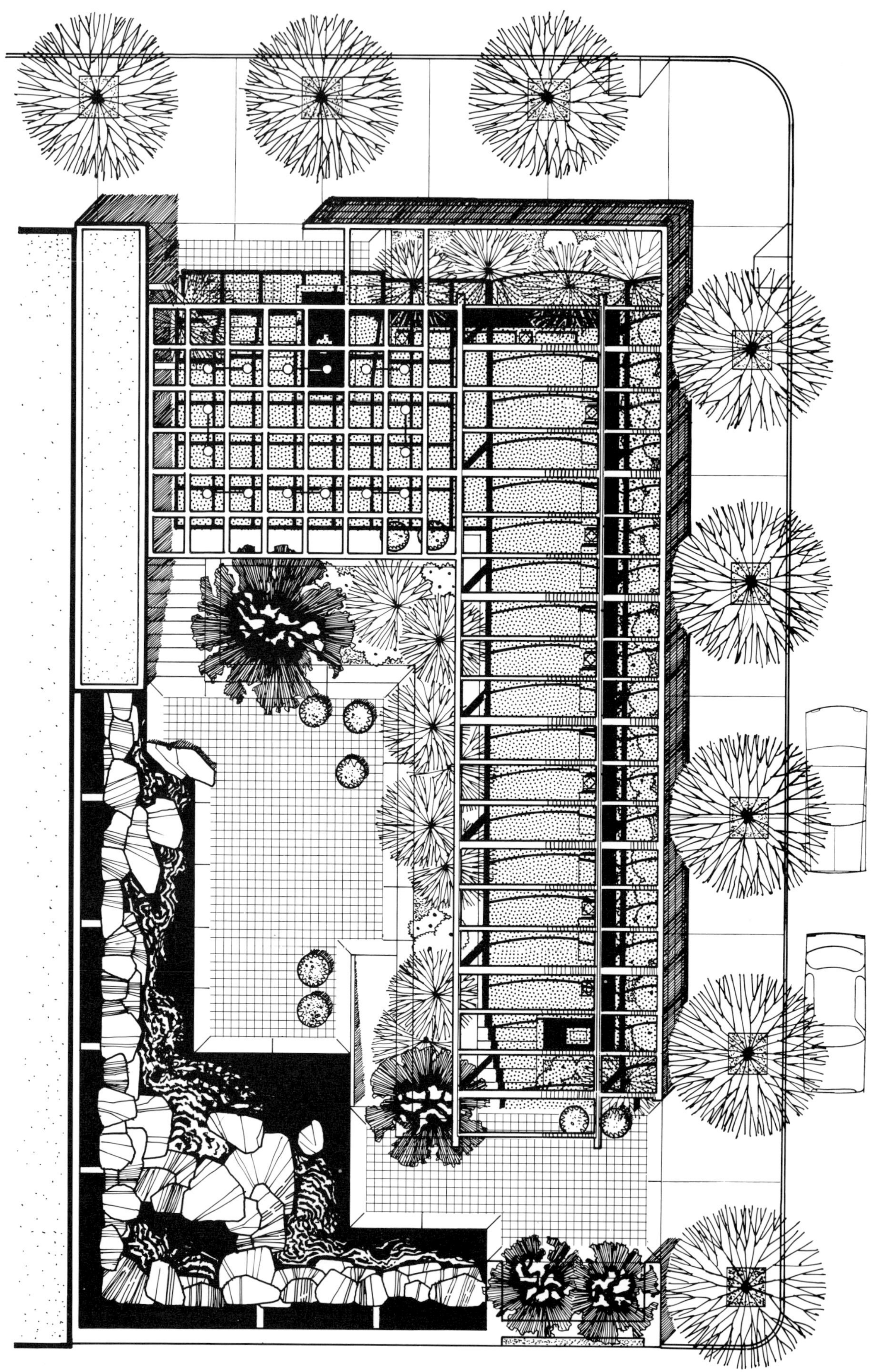

Plan for the Waterfall Garden. South entrance at the lower right.

WATERFALL GARDEN
Seattle, Washington

Design firm: Sasaki Associates

Located in the Pioneer Square Historic District of downtown Seattle, this small park measures 60 by 108 feet. Its focal point is a waterfall in one corner where two granite walls join. The cascading water creates a background sound that insulates the viewer from surrounding city noises. Even though quite small the park has several levels and spaces where visitors can sit, relax and enjoy a snack or lunch. There are several areas for trees, shrubs and flowers to provide a natural setting.

A glass and oxidized steel trellis provides protection from rain, but the area retains a feeling of spaciousness. Lighting and radiant heat for comfort during evening hours and colder weather.

South entrance and view of rock waterfalls.

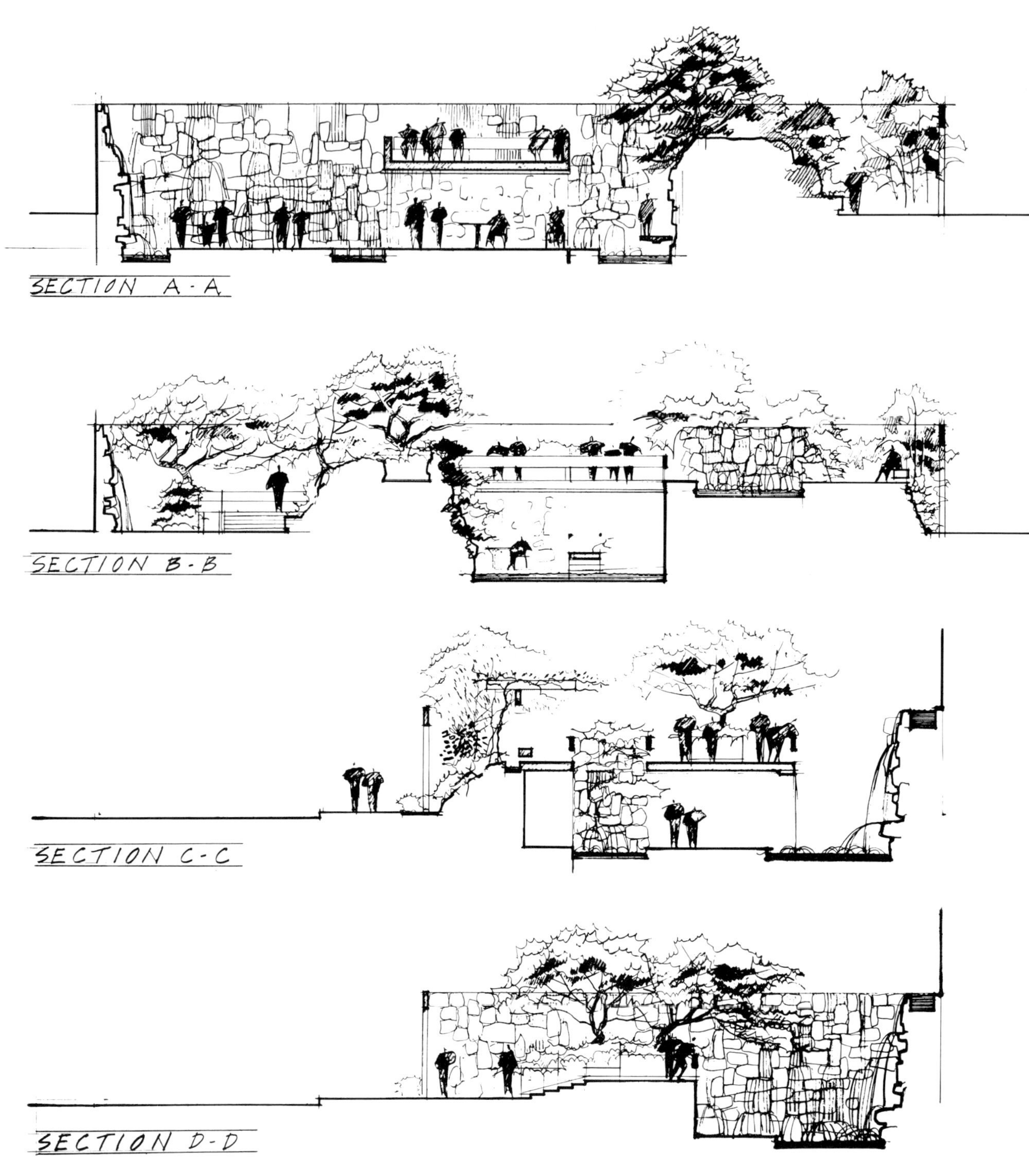

Designer's cross sections through Waterfall Garden.

Looking towards the waterfalls from near the east entrance.

Closeup of the waterfalls.

Raised dining area with shelter along the south side of the Garden Waterfalls.

Small sculptural fountain on the upper level.

FORECOURT FOUNTAIN
Portland, Oregon

Design firm: Lawrence Halprin & Associates

As part of Portland's urban renewal program a complete city block was set aside for this park. With streets on all four sides and the resultant traffic noise, the designer recessed a major portion of the park, enclosed it with plant materials and created an island of solitude with the sound of cascading water. The upper levels consists of a series of shallow pools of water in which visitors to the park can play and cool off. Open paving provides sunning space. The lower level can be viewed from a series of steps in an amphitheater-like effect.

Forecourt Fountain as seen from the top of a parking garage in 1970, 16 years before the rest of the photographs of this park were taken.

East entrance of the park from the top of the waterfalls.

At the east entrance looking west.

Face of the waterfalls.

Lighting provides a special mood to Forecourt Fountain at night.

At the right, out of view, is an entrance that allows visitors to walk behind and under the Waterfall.

LOVEJOY PARK
Portland, Oregon

**Design firms: Lawrence Halprin & Associates
Moore & Turnbull**

In the redevelopment of a portion of downtown Portland, this one acre park occupies a site near several high rise buildings. The site is sloping and lends itself to the terrace effect the designer created. The whole park is a series of angles and the contour-like effect in the fountain, the cascades and the surrounding terraces creates an interesting design result. Water at the rate of 3,100 gallons per minute rushes down the central cascade. The cascade can be viewed from several different directions as well as from above.

The shelter is also angular in design and is constructed of lattice, truss, and copper shingles.

This fountain with its sculptural forms and terraces form the heart of Lovejoy Park.

Two more views of the fountain.

Park structure adds harmonious form to the fountain. Color is provided by flowers in the planters.

Concrete sculpture and waterfalls.

FREEWAY PARK
Seattle, Washington

Design firm: Lawrence Halprin & Associates
(designer: Angela Danadjieva)

As the name of the park implies, it is associated with a freeway. To improve the aesthetics of downtown Seattle where the freeway slashed through and provide pedestrian access, a park was built like a lid or bridge over the freeway. Consisting of five acres, it is a series of modules with numerous planters and several waterfalls. The plants have softened the effect of all the concrete that was used and added green to the city environment where the park is located. The sound of 28,000 gallons of water per minute falling over tall concrete cliffs located over the median of the freeway completely masks the noise of the freeway underneath.

Freeway Park bridges the interstate which runs alongside downtown Seattle.

Low sculpture and waterfalls.

High waterfalls

Another of the several waterfalls in Freeway Park.

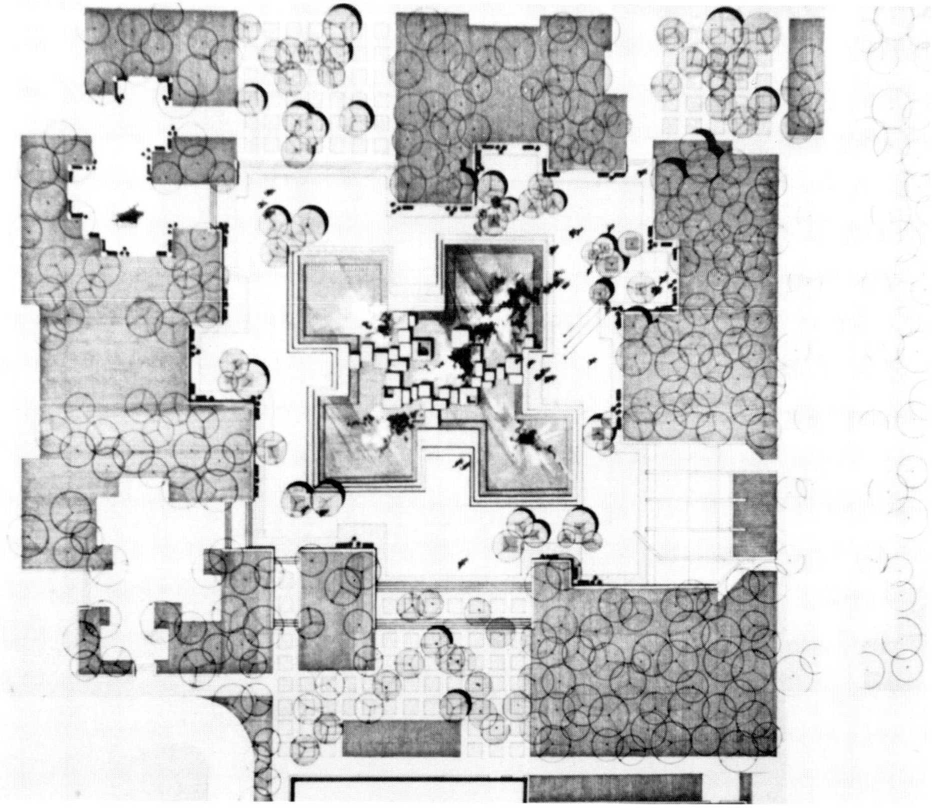

Master Plan for Freimann Square.

FREIMANN SQUARE
Fort Wayne, Indiana

Design firms: Browning Day Mullins Dierdorf
Strauss Associates

The site for this park was created through urban renewal activities. Four blocks of very old buildings were demolished to create room for the park. It is bounded on the north by an elevated railroad, on the west by the City-County Building, on the east by a new auditorium designed by Louis Kahn, and on the south by existing retail buildings still part of the downtown area.

The design concept was to provide an oasis in the center of urban development by creating a large pool as a focal point, and to soften traffic noise with mounds and the sounds of water. In addition, a display garden for annuals and perennials was to be created.

Main entrances to the site were established on the southeast and southwest corners to correspond to the traffic signals. Near the southeast entrance which has the least traffic is the "display garden" with its quiet area of benches and massed flowers backed by mounds and flowering trees. The main entrance at the southwest focuses on a bronze equestrian statue of the City's namesake, General 'Mad' Anthony Wayne. Other entrances on the west and east sides are on axis with the City-County Building and the auditorium.

The center of the park is recessed below street level and with the peripheral mounds, the central area is visually and aurally isolated from city noises. The fountain has five different sequenced effects and is the focal point of the center of the park.

The pavement is largely brick with a grid pattern created with concrete. There is sufficient paved area to facilitate a number of community events within the park and adjacent to the fountain.

The large fountain is the central focal point of the whole park. In the rear is the historic county courthouse. A new city office building is on the right.

Central fountain.

Designer's original concept.

Concept for a sitting area.

Sitting area as built.

Perennial garden in concept form and as built.

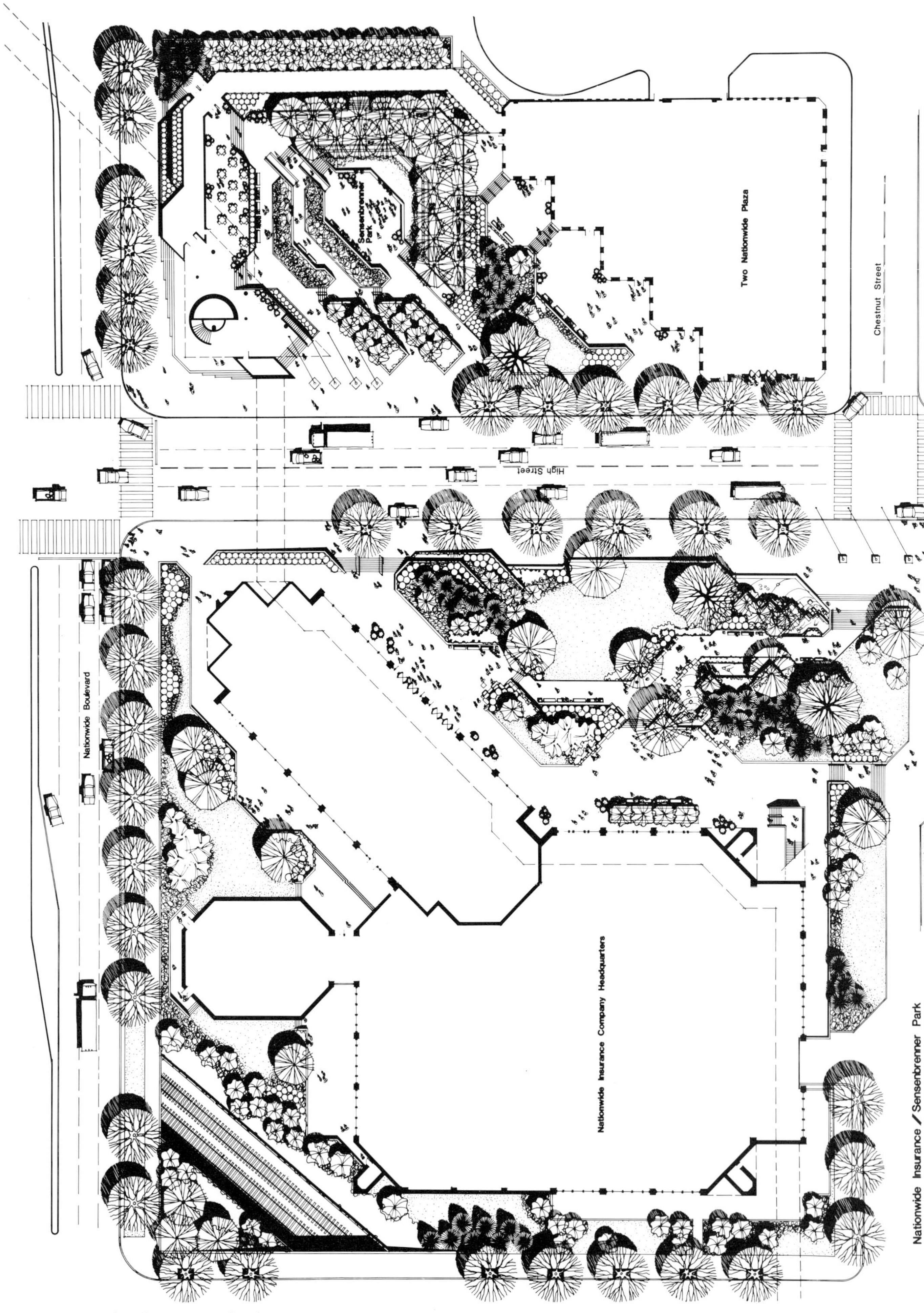

Master Plan for Nationwide Plaza.

NATIONWIDE PLAZA
Columbus, Ohio

**Design firms: Sasaki Associates
Abramovitz, Harris, Kingsland**

Nationwide Plaza is an 1-1/2 acre site that is part of an urban revitalization area in downtown Columbus. It is built over underground office space on a structural deck-top. Artificial soil conditions surrounding high-rise buildings and resultant shadows and wind patterns required special selection and placement of plant materials.

The plaza design creates a variety of spaces and vistas on the sloping site. Wooded knolls and open glades, functional walkways, plazas and seating areas all provide an enjoyable respite for employees during lunch hours and for downtown special events.

Taking advantage of the sloping site, a watercourse was designed to meander through the plaza, bringing the natural sounds of a rural setting to the urban environment. Starting as a spring at the top of the plaza, water spills over ledges, streams through the plaza, and cascades into a large pool at the plaza base.

Natural rose-colored, split-face granite, seasonal plantings, and a diversity of textures provide an ever-changing scene throughout the year.

Pathways, sitting areas and fountain.

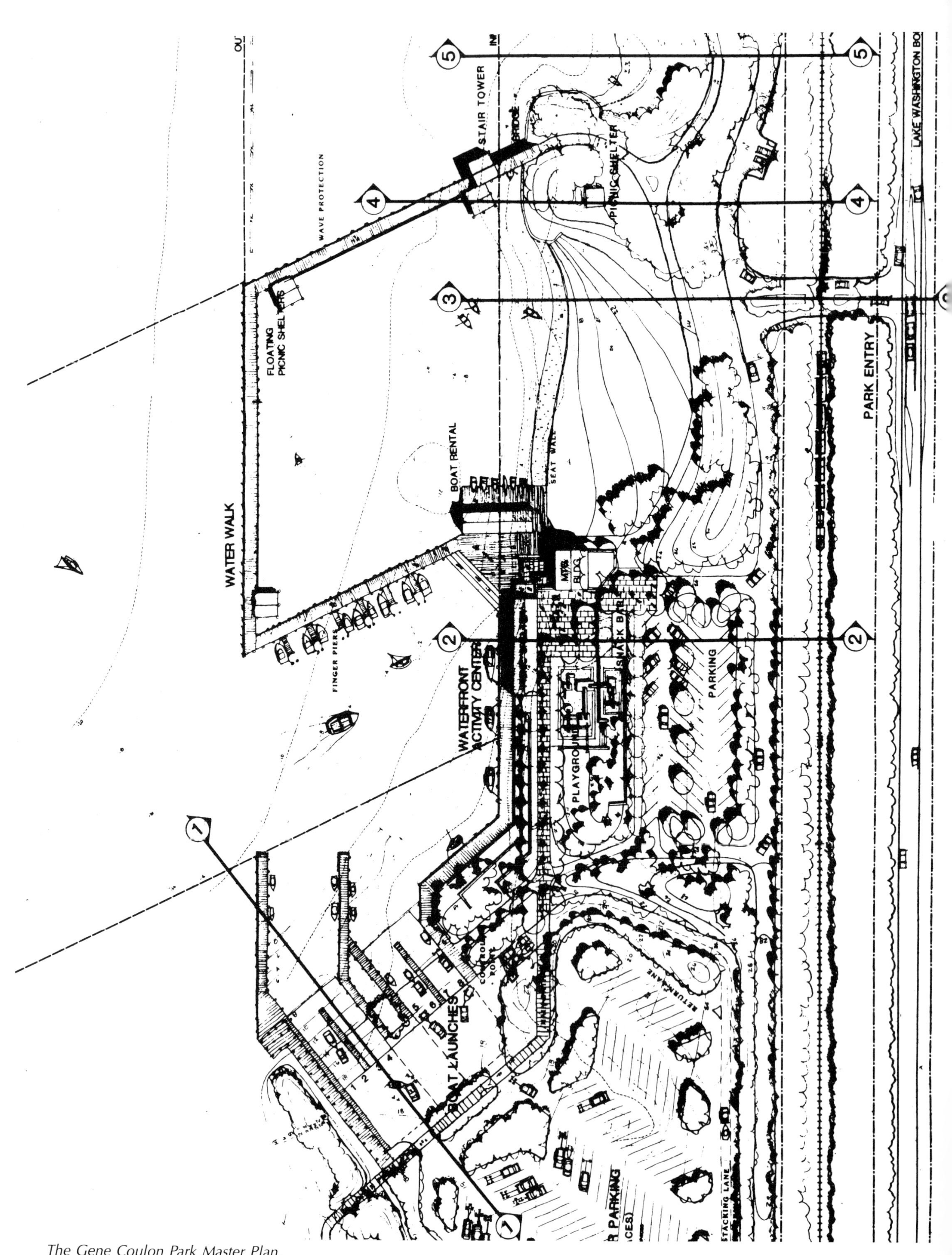

The Gene Coulon Park Master Plan.

GENE COULON PARK
Renton, Washington

Design firm: Jones & Jones

Gene Coulon Park stretches for a mile along the shore of Lake Washington. This 34 acre site formerly had been used for logging, log storage, coal shipping, wartime ship fitting, and dumping of construction debris. The water-oriented design reflects the input of needs and desires expressed by the citizens of Renton. The park provides family recreation and a range of active and passive uses from power boating to nature study. A waterfront activity center at the south end of the park includes boat launching, day moorage, boat rental, and a restaurant. To the north, a floating "waterwalk" allows people to walk out onto Lake Washington for fishing, viewing and picnicking. This encloses a protected area for use of wind surfing lessons and rented paddle boats. A foot trail winds through the naturalized north half of the park where industrial debris and ditches have been replaced by hills, a renovated stream and marsh, cobble beaches, and naturalistic planting of trees and shrubs.

Salmon spawning requirements determined the shoreline profile and the location of several elements of the plan. Building designs acknowledge the industrial character of adjoining land uses and the traditional forms of turn-of-the-century waterfront parks.

Picnic shelter with viewing tower and piers.

Walkway with floating pier.

Viewing point north along Lake Washington.

Beach and raised picnic area with shelter.

Closeup of viewpoint.

Timber seating is warm and dry at edge of lake.

Stream inlet and bridge along the hiking trail.

Sheltered area for practicing wind surfing.

Floating picnic platform.

ATLANTIC OCEAN
MAIN BEACH
SURFING BEACH
BOARDWALK ACCESS TO BEACH
LIFEGUARD STATION
VOLLEYBALL
LIFEGUARD STATION
BOARDWALK ACCESS TO BEACH
DUNE REFURBISHMENT
EXERCISE APPARATUS
DUNE REFURBISHMENT
BOARDWALK ACCESS TO BEACH
EMERGENCY SERVICE VEHICULAR ACCESS TO BEACH
OVERLOOK SHELTERS
OVERLOOK SHELTERS
SHOWERS AND CLEANING STATION TYPICAL
INTERPRETIVE SHELTER
TO COUNTY PARK NATURE AREA
PARKING 47 CARS
HNDCP
CONCESSION BUILDING
PARKING 95 CARS
MENS RESTROOM
WOMENS RESTROOM
BATH HOUSE
BATH HOUSE
GROUP PICNIC AREA
SERVICE YARD
RETENTION BASIN
GATEHOUSE
EXIT
PARK ENTRANCE
HNDCP
HNDCP
MOTORCYCLE PARKING
EXIT ONLY
A1A
PARKING 146 CARS
RETENTION BASIN SCREEN
PROPOSED ROADWAY
NORTH
SCALE: 1 : 40
5 20 40   100
0 10 30 50
BOYNTON BEACH PARK
BOYNTON BEACH,   FLORIDA
EDWARD D. STONE JR. AND ASSOCIATES P.A.
SITE PLANNERS   LANDSCAPE ARCHITECTS
FORT LAUDERDALE,   FLORIDA
ARCHITECTURAL DESIGN GROUP, INCORPORATED
ARCHITECTS
FORT LAUDERDALE,   FLORIDA
QUIBLE AND ASSOCIATES OF FLORIDA INC.
CONSULTING ENGINEERS   LAND SURVEYORS
FORT LAUDERDALE,   FLORIDA
MASTER PLAN
DATE: 7 OCTOBER 1980
SCALE: 1 : 40
DRAWN: JWM S.S.
SHEET: 1

BOYNTON BEACH OCEANFRONT PARK
Boynton Beach, Florida

Design firm: Edward D. Stone, Jr. & Associates

Boynton Beach Oceanfront Park is an example of the rehabilitation of an existing city park. While the City was looking for a simple solution to delapidated or inadequate facilities, the designers found in evaluating the site that the primary dune had gradually eroded due to uncontrolled foot traffic and wind erosion, a direct result of the absence of vegetative cover. It was of paramount importance to rebuild this dune and stabilize it with native dune vegetation. Because most the park users were elderly, ease of access and barrier free circulation were desirable and not available in the existing park.

Views into the park from the road and surrounding neighborhoods have been improved in the new design. The perception of the city by passers-by has been greatly enhanced. The park is now barrier free and a wheelchair user can circulate from any point within the parking area, onto and along the entire boardwalk system and even over the dune to the beach by way of two ramped boardwalk systems connecting the upper boardwalk with the beach below. The dune has been restored, protected and enhanced and a very high level of use is maintained with no damage to this restored coastal ecosystem.

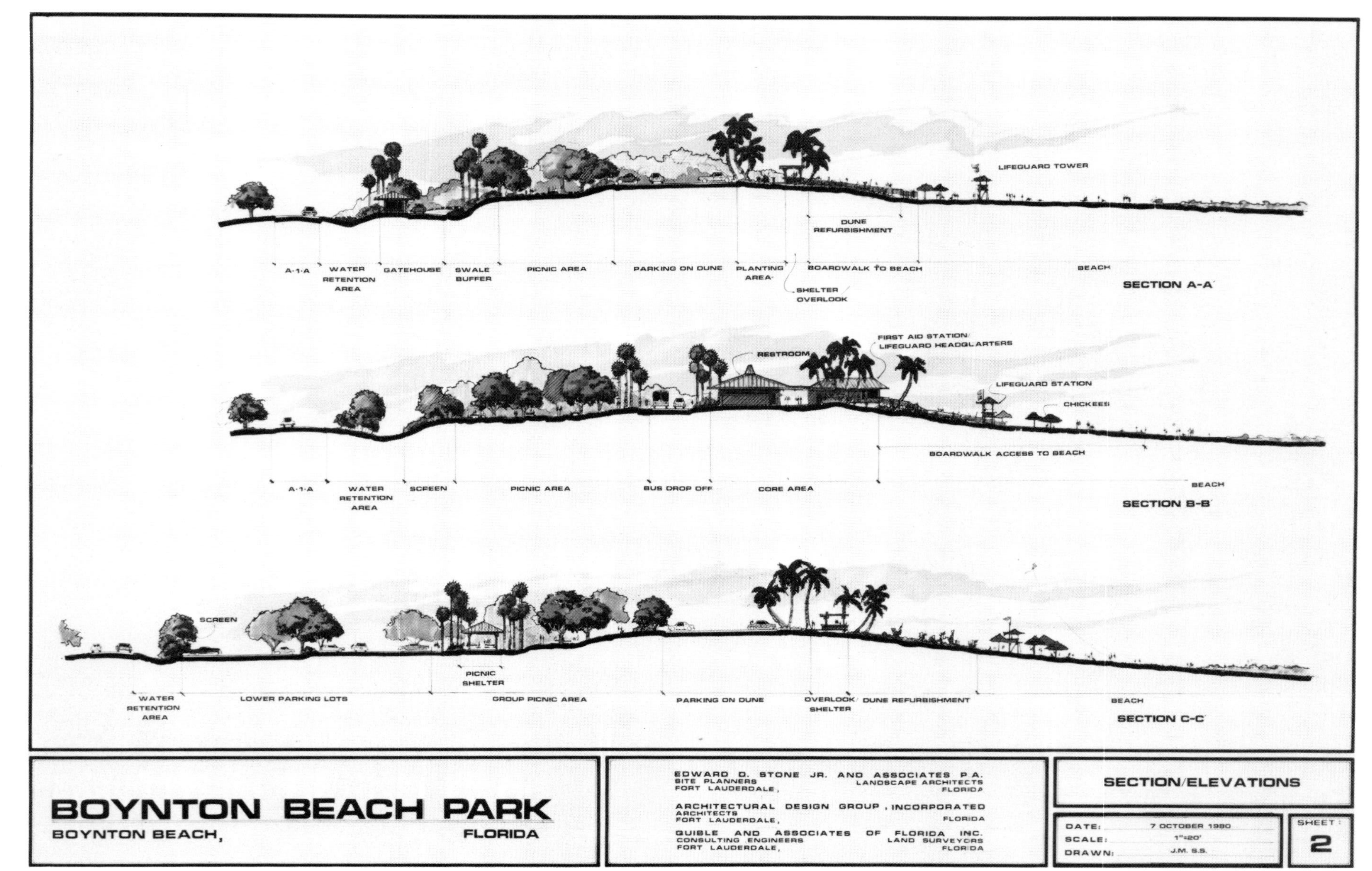

BOYNTON BEACH PARK

BOYNTON BEACH,   FLORIDA

EDWARD D. STONE JR. AND ASSOCIATES P.A.
SITE PLANNERS   LANDSCAPE ARCHITECTS
FORT LAUDERDALE,   FLORIDA

ARCHITECTURAL DESIGN GROUP, INCORPORATED
ARCHITECTS
FORT LAUDERDALE,   FLORIDA

QUIBLE AND ASSOCIATES OF FLORIDA INC.
CONSULTING ENGINEERS   LAND SURVEYORS
FORT LAUDERDALE,   FLORIDA

SECTION/ELEVATIONS

DATE: 7 OCTOBER 1990
SCALE: 1"=20'
DRAWN: J.M. S.S.

SHEET: 2

Boardwalks and covered viewing points along Boynton Beach.

Views of Boynton Beach Park facilities and playground.

GREENFIELD PARK
Wilmington, North Carolina

Design firm: Edward D. Stone, Jr. & Associates

This is an existing 200 acre park which has been refurbished. Most of the park (175 acres) consisted of a man-made lake and surrounding shoreline areas. Facilities which were designed for this park included roads, parking, pedestrian and bike circulation, concessions, restrooms, boat rental, picnic facilities, playgrounds, gardens, game areas, nature areas, amphitheater and general utility and site improvements.

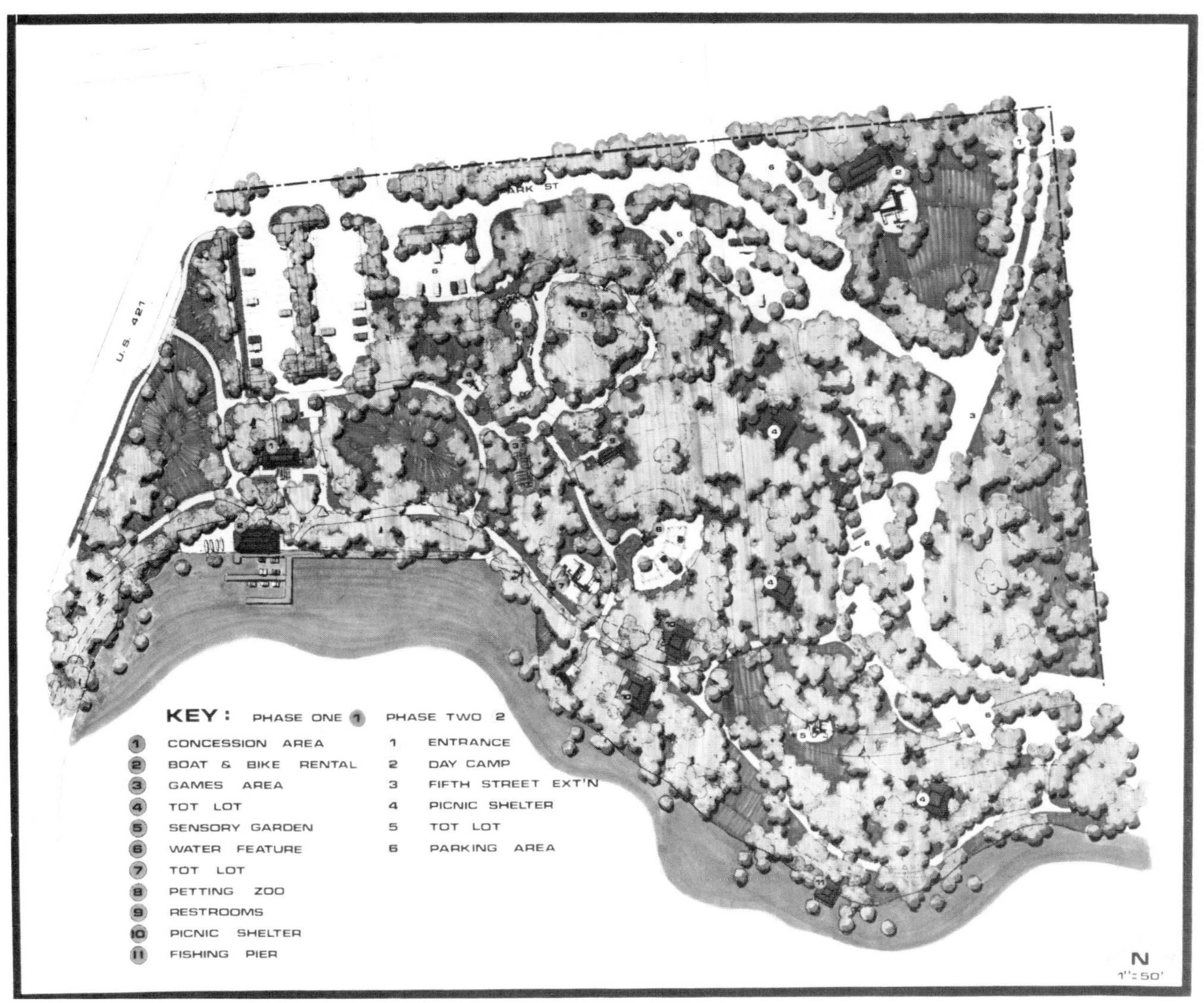

Master Plan.

SECTION C-C'

SECTION D-D'

SITE SECTIONS

GREENFIELD PARK

WILMINGTON, NORTH CAROLINA

PREPARED FOR

PARKS & RECREATION DEPARTMENT
CITY OF WILMINGTON, NORTH CAROLINA

Edward D. Stone, Jr. and Associates, P.A.
Planners and Landscape Architects

EDSA

Existing lake with new boat facilities.

Picnic shelters and playground at Greenfield Park.

SPANISH RIVER PARK
Boca Raton, Florida

**Design firms: Edward D. Stone, Jr. & Associates
Shoup, McKingley, Roll, Johnson & Barrows.**

This park is a working example of how a site can be designed for public use and preserve existing ecological conditions in an atmosphere of natural beauty. It lies between 1800 feet of Atlantic Ocean beachfront and the Intracoastal Waterway, where its shoreline follows the channel of an old, shallow fresh-water stream once called Spanish River. The park covers 45 acres and is accessible by both car and boat.

The city-operated facility has parking for 600 cars, several picnic areas with shelters and barbecues, nature trails and boat dockage. Pedestrian underpasses beneath North Ocean Boulevard connect the park proper with the public beach, while a 58 foot observation tower on the edge of the Intracoastal lagoon provides a panoramic view of the area.

Designed to conform to rather than alter the existing terrain, everything added by man blends with the environment as unobtrusively as possible. Coral rock forms the base of most structures; old railroad ties serve as parking bumpers; pine bark covers the paths; and the weathered wood used in sign posts, lamp poles and buildings helps them blend into the background.

Every effort was made to preserve the original vegetation. Where it was necessary to add to the existing landscape, only material complementary to that already growing and adaptable to the wind and salt conditions prevalent in the area was used. Seasonal plantings add special interest and give separation to different areas of intensive use.

The plan reflects a design solution which avoids vehicular-pedestrian conflict within the grounds. Parking spaces are located around existing stands of trees to screen parking areas from view, as well as avoid the unattractive aspect of unbroken asphalt sheeting. The prime goal was to assure that the need for parking and circulation did not detract from the naturalistic setting.

boat launching
intracoastal waterway
natural area
nature area
Board walk
atlantic ocean
SPANISH RIVER PARK
N

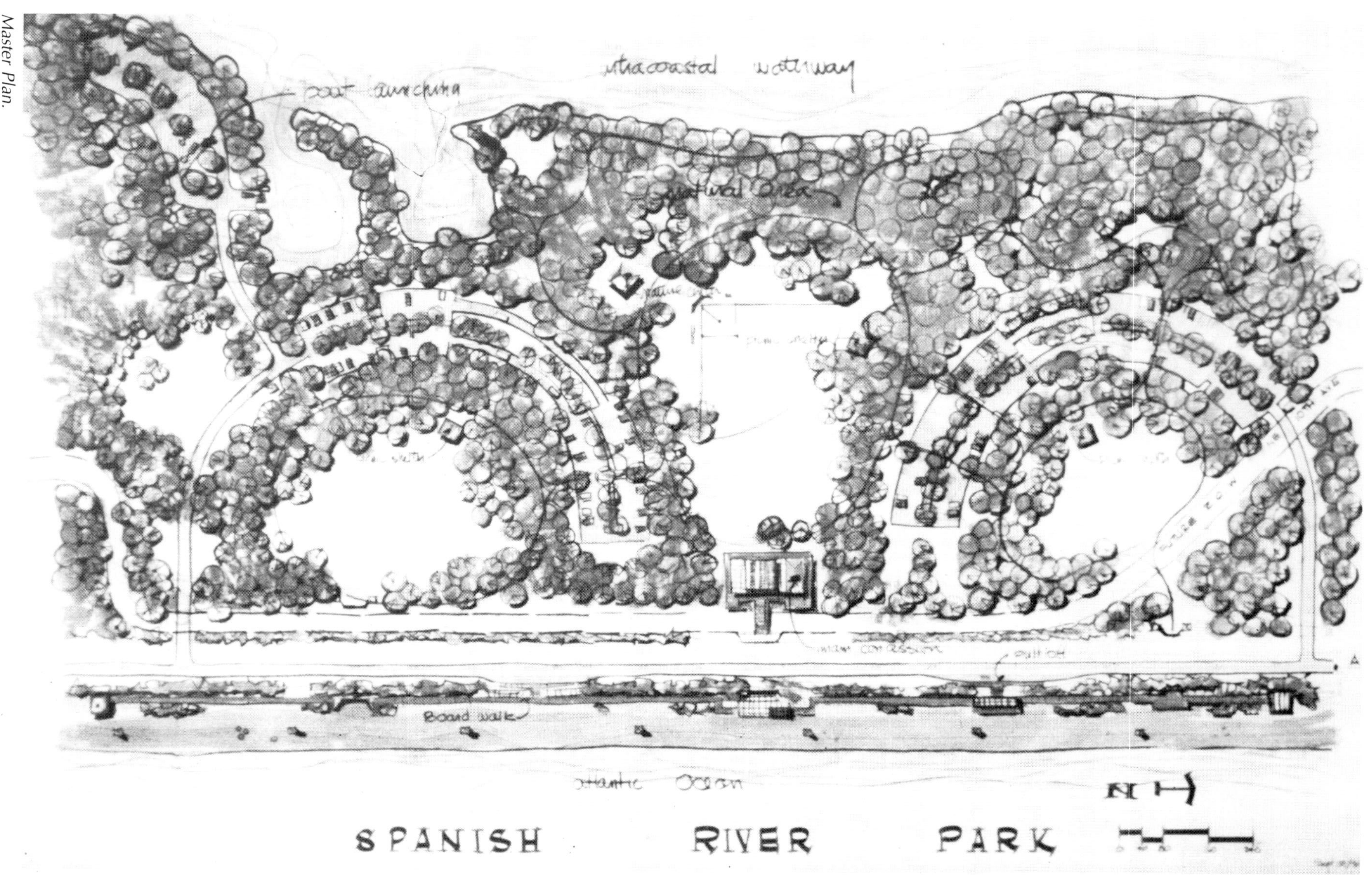

Master Plan.

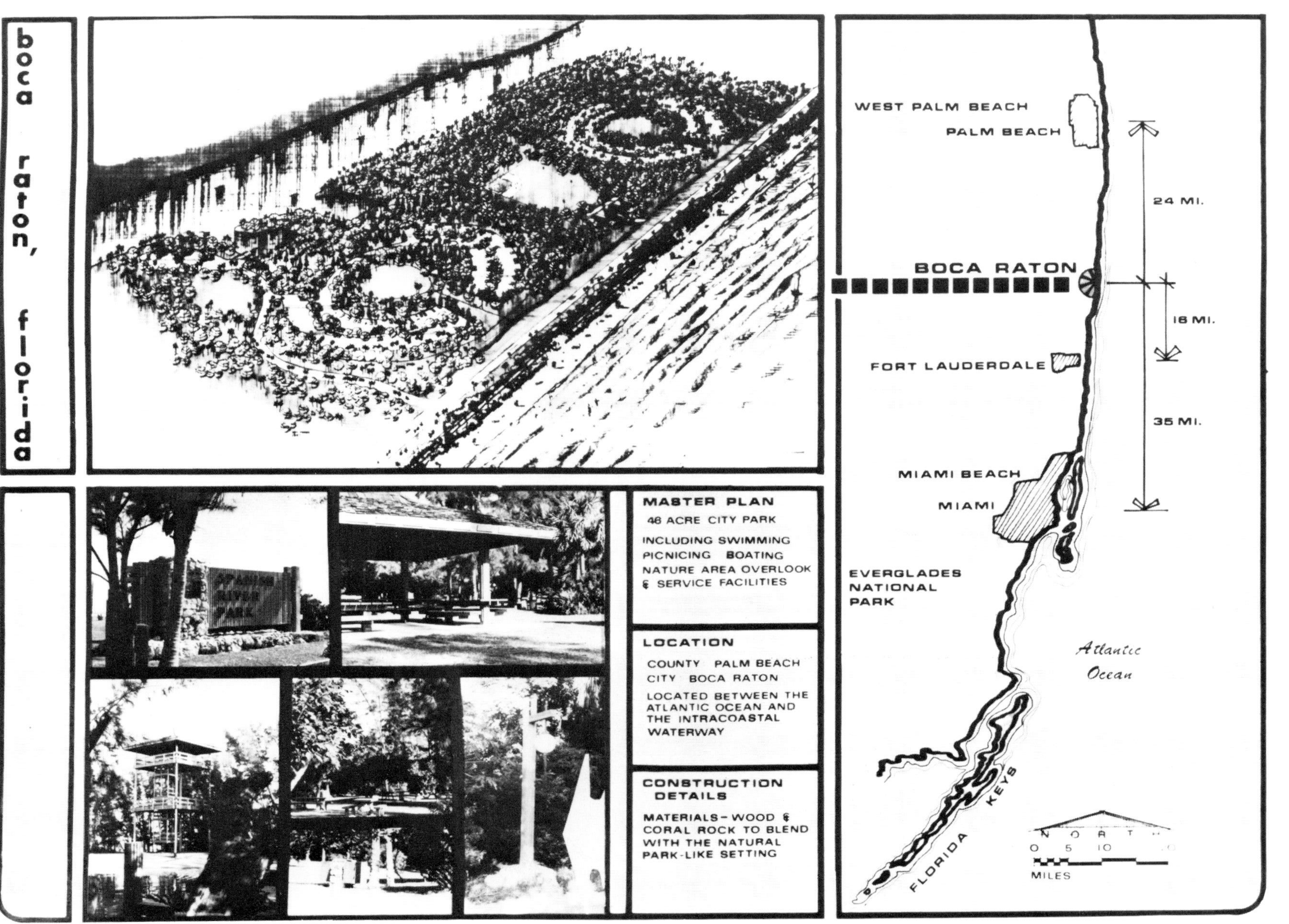

boca raton, florida

WEST PALM BEACH
PALM BEACH
24 MI.
BOCA RATON
18 MI.
FORT LAUDERDALE
35 MI.
MIAMI BEACH
MIAMI
EVERGLADES NATIONAL PARK
Atlantic Ocean
FLORIDA KEYS
NORTH
0 5 10
MILES

MASTER PLAN
48 ACRE CITY PARK
INCLUDING SWIMMING PICNICING BOATING NATURE AREA OVERLOOK & SERVICE FACILITIES

LOCATION
COUNTY PALM BEACH
CITY BOCA RATON
LOCATED BETWEEN THE ATLANTIC OCEAN AND THE INTRACOASTAL WATERWAY

CONSTRUCTION DETAILS
MATERIALS—WOOD & CORAL ROCK TO BLEND WITH THE NATURAL PARK-LIKE SETTING

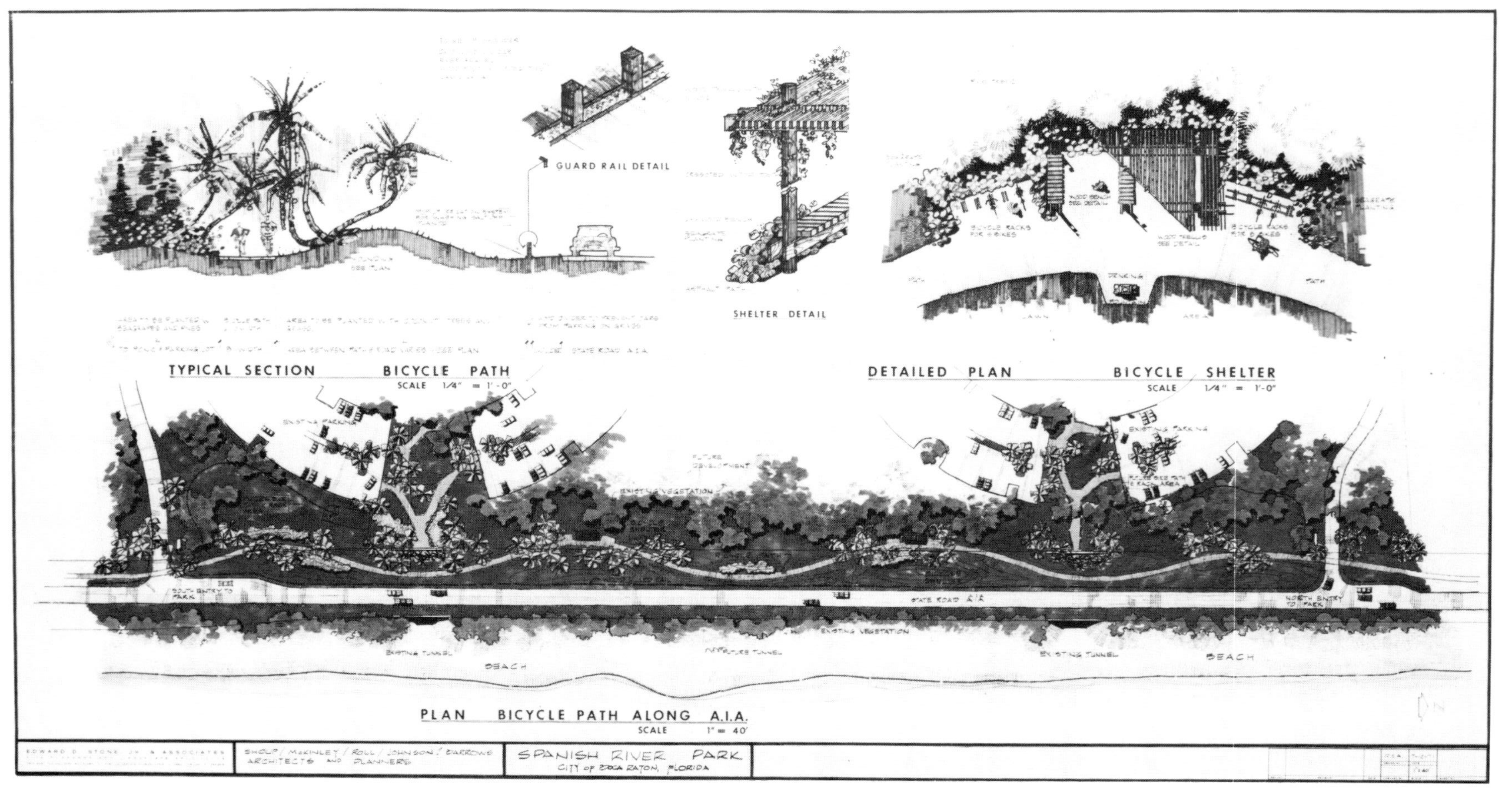
GUARD RAIL DETAIL
SHELTER DETAIL
TYPICAL SECTION   BICYCLE PATH
SCALE 1/4" = 1'-0"
DETAILED PLAN   BICYCLE SHELTER
SCALE 1/4" = 1'-0"
BICYCLE RACKS FOR BIKES
BICYCLE RACKS FOR BIKES
PLAN   BICYCLE PATH ALONG A.I.A.
SCALE 1" = 40'
STATE ROAD A.I.A.
SOUTH ENTRY TO PARK
NORTH ENTRY TO PARK
EXISTING TUNNEL
EXISTING TUNNEL
BEACH
BEACH
EXISTING VEGETATION
FUTURE DEVELOPMENT
EXISTING PARKING
EDWARD D. STONE JR. & ASSOCIATES
SHEP / McKINLEY / ROLL / JOHNSON / DARROW
ARCHITECTS AND PLANNERS
SPANISH RIVER PARK
CITY OF BOCA RATON, FLORIDA

Observation tower and intracoastal waterway in foreground. Beach and Atlantic Ocean in background.

Picnic sites and observation tower.

Picnic sites and hiking trail at Spanish River Park.

CANAL PARK
Akron, Ohio

Design firms: Environmental Planning & Design
Lawrence Halprin & Associates
Glaus, Pyle, Schomer, Burns & DeHaven
James H. Bassett

This canal runs through an area of Akron just south of the central business district. For decades is was little more than an open storm sewer and a threat to public health. During urban renewal it was turned into a pleasant, scenic, recreational facility. It became the heart of a new housing and commercial district.

The canal was widened to keep it shallow for safety reasons. A recirculation system was added and the sides lined with concrete. The total length of the canal is one-half mile with an adjacent 8 acre park which includes tree-lined walkways, benches, planters, concrete water sculpture, observation platforms and wooden bridges.

Water sculpture adjacent to play area.

Pedestrian bridge over the canal.

Observation tower and sitting area along edge of canal.

Playground at Canal Park.

3 GUADALUPE RIVER PARK, LOOKING SOUTH FROM WEST SANTA CLARA STREET (ZONE C)

GUADALUPE RIVER PARK
San Jose, California

Design firm: EDAW, Inc.

The City of San Jose is located in the ''Silicon Valley'' where many high-tech companies are located, and there is considerable growth. Like many cities the downtown area is being revitalized with urban renewal programs. Three miles of the Guadalupe River flows through downtown San Jose and provides an opportunity for a linear park. The design was coordinated with the U. S. Army Corps of Engineers who is responsible for flood alleviation work. The intent of the design was to create a water-oriented ''natural'' park oasis in the heart of downtown, and weave the image of the park beyond its precise physical boundaries into and around major redevelopment projects proposed on adjacent lands.

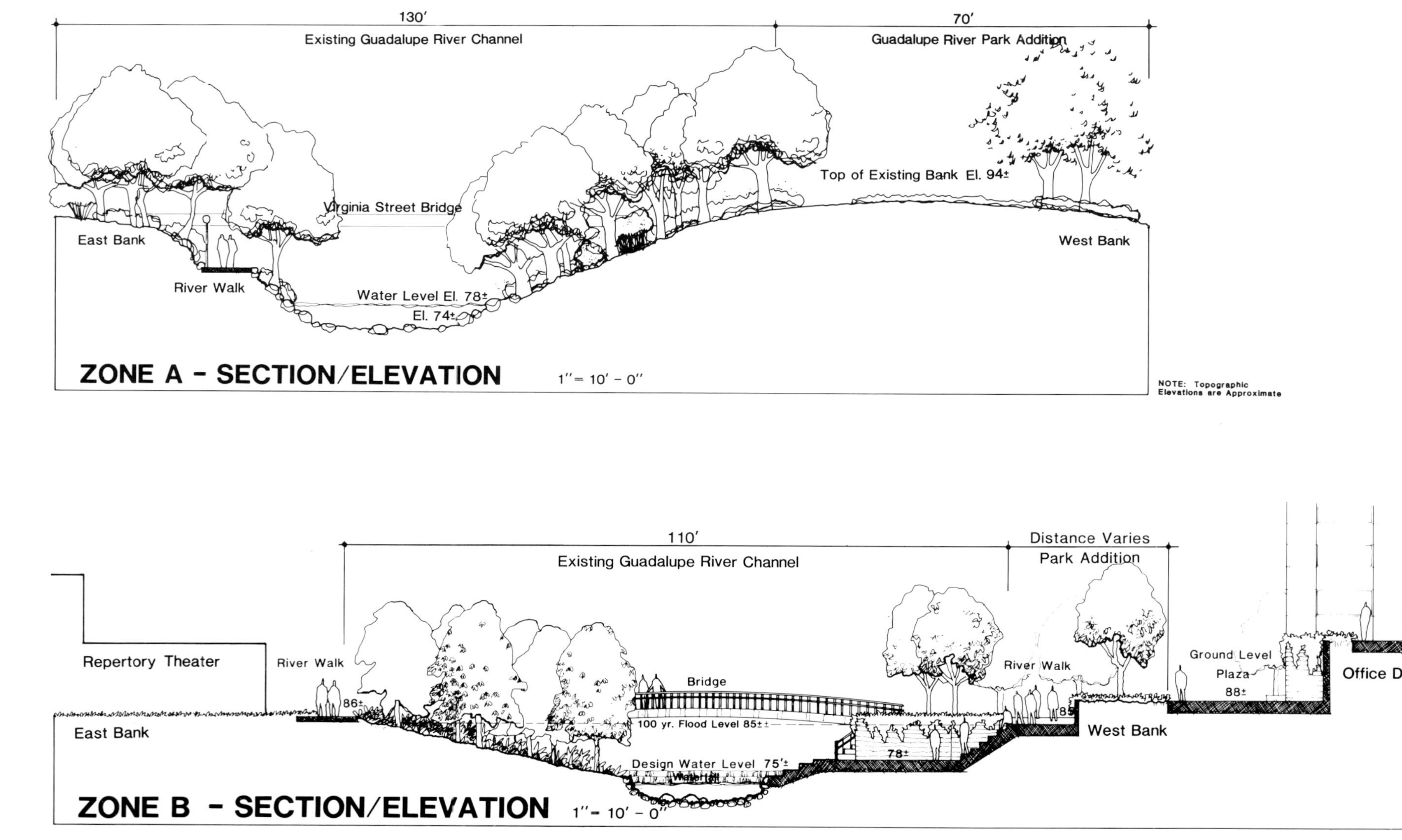

130'
Existing Guadalupe River Channel
70'
Guadalupe River Park Addition
Top of Existing Bank El. 94±
East Bank
West Bank
Virginia Street Bridge
River Walk
Water Level El. 78±
El. 74±
ZONE A - SECTION/ELEVATION
1" = 10' - 0"
NOTE: Topographic Elevations are Approximate
110'
Existing Guadalupe River Channel
Distance Varies
Park Addition
Repertory Theater
River Walk
Bridge
River Walk
Ground Level Plaza 88±
Office De
86±
100 yr. Flood Level 85±
East Bank
Design Water Level 75'±
Waterfall
78±
85
West Bank
ZONE B - SECTION/ELEVATION
1" - 10' - 0"

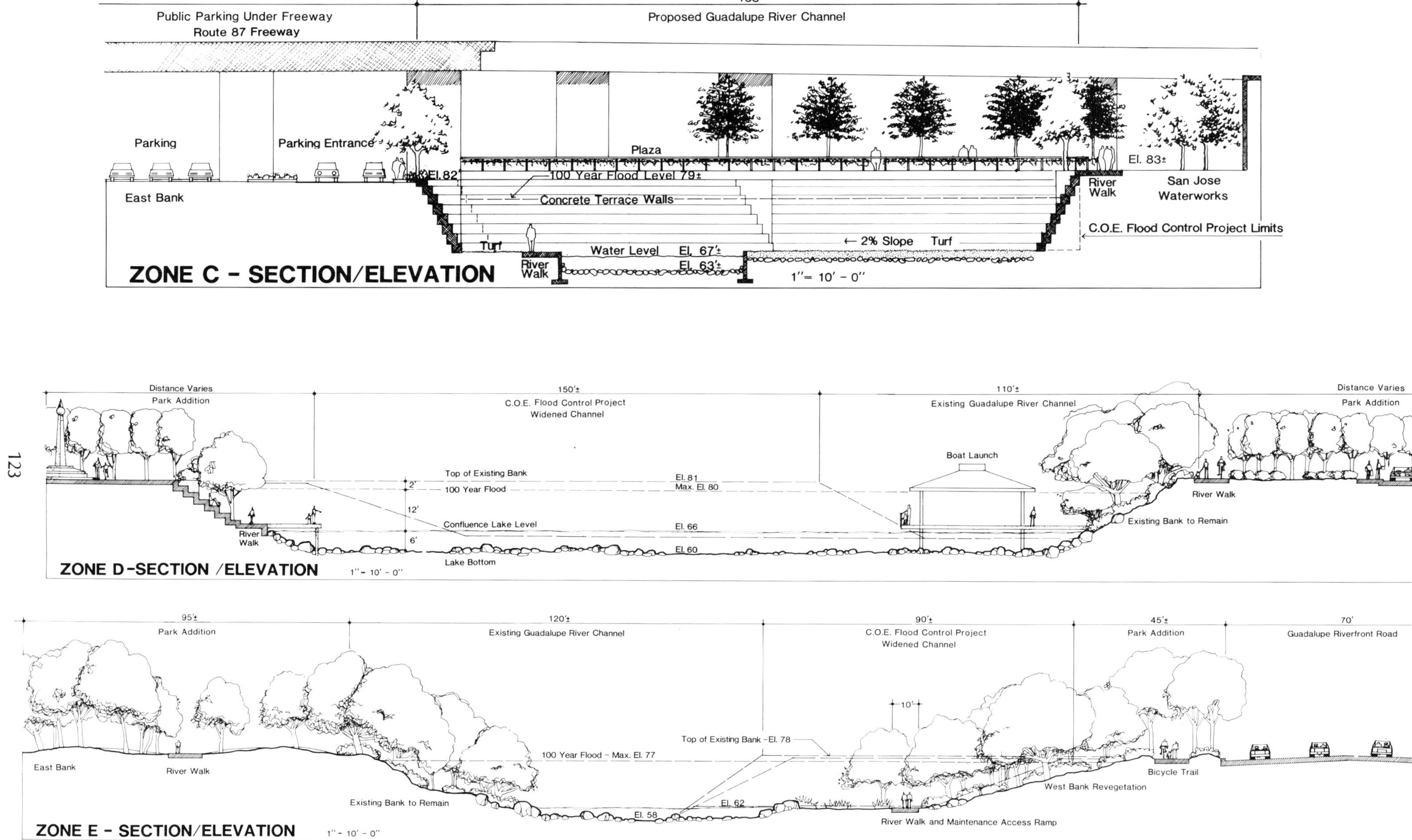

138'
Public Parking Under Freeway
Route 87 Freeway
Proposed Guadalupe River Channel
Parking
Parking Entrance
Plaza
El. 82
El. 83±
100 Year Flood Level 79±
Concrete Terrace Walls
River Walk
San Jose Waterworks
East Bank
Turf
Water Level   El. 67'±
El. 63'±
River Walk
← 2% Slope   Turf
C.O.E. Flood Control Project Limits
1" = 10' - 0"
ZONE C - SECTION/ELEVATION
Distance Varies
Park Addition
150'±
C.O.E. Flood Control Project
Widened Channel
110'±
Existing Guadalupe River Channel
Distance Varies
Park Addition
Boat Launch
Top of Existing Bank
2'
100 Year Flood
El. 81
Max. El. 80
River Walk
12'
Confluence Lake Level
El. 66
Existing Bank to Remain
River Walk
6'
El. 60
Lake Bottom
ZONE D-SECTION /ELEVATION
1" - 10' - 0"
123
95'±
Park Addition
120'±
Existing Guadalupe River Channel
90'±
C.O.E. Flood Control Project
Widened Channel
45'±
Park Addition
70'
Guadalupe Riverfront Road
10'
Top of Existing Bank – El. 78
East Bank
River Walk
100 Year Flood – Max. El. 77
Bicycle Trail
Existing Bank to Remain
El. 58
El. 62
West Bank Revegetation
River Walk and Maintenance Access Ramp
ZONE E - SECTION/ELEVATION
1" - 10' - 0"

Concept for development of Guadalupe River Park.

CEDAR RIVER TRAIL
Renton, Washington

Design firm: Jongejan/Gerrard/McNeal

The Cedar River flows from a rural/woodland landscape through the urban core of the city and a few residential neighborhoods and into a large industrial area before emptying into Lake Washington. Like many streams it has been affected by increased siltation, floodwaters following winter storms, and low summer flows with high in-stream temperatures. Altered flow characteristics threatened the fish population as salmon use this river for spawning. To maintain adequate channel capacity, the City of Renton had been forced to annually dredge the river.

In the past the aesthetic and recreational opportunities of the river has been largely ignored. Parking lots for industrial workers crowded the edges of the stream. There was a dump site for surplus gravel. Other portions of the river were inaccessible to potential users because of thick tangles of rat-infested blackberry vines and scrub vegetation.

The main goals in the design of the Cedar River Trail system were to improve the flow characteristics of the river, eliminate the annual dredging and reclaim the area for public use by making the river the focus of the community.

Of the 4.8 miles of proposed trail the first 1.5 miles have been completed and are illustrated here. This section links the Renton City Hall with the industrial area adjacent to Lake Washington. Through the urban core with a mix of small commercial business, office buildings and single family housing, the corridor of the river is narrow. To improve low flow characteristics of the river, a walkway was constructed in the existing channel close to the summer flow level of the river. This channelizing edge will confine the low flow enough to maintain adequate water depth and velocity. The high retaining walls along the walkway will increase the high flow channel capacity and quickly move flood water through this developed area.

As it passes through the urban core, the river is bridged by several roads. The trail minimizes auto/pedestrian conflict. Ramps are provided for access to the handicapped at all major access points. The trail links existing parks, City Hall, the library, the high school stadium, and Senior Citizen's Center. Numerous benches along the trail provide rest stops and lunching areas for nearby workers and residents.

Through the industrial area of the river, the corridor broadens and the river has fewer functional problems. The channel is deep and flood waters are no longer a threat to nearby homes and businesses. The land area devoted to recreation is increased to match the scale of the surroundings. This includes broad green meadows and massive tree plantings. Facilities include a twenty station parcourse, children's play area, basketball courts and horseshoes. There are several areas for picnicking and a small scale boat launch is available for sports fishermen.

This section of trail is near City Hall and the urban core where the river channel was narrowed to improve summer flow.

Ramp up from the trail to the Senior Citizens' Center in the background.

Senior Citizens' Center at one road-trail intersection.

Further north on the trail are restrooms and play facilities.

Picnic shelter and play area near the north end of the trail.

Exercise station and trail.

A point where the river widens and there is easy access to the water. Boeing Airplane facilities to the right.

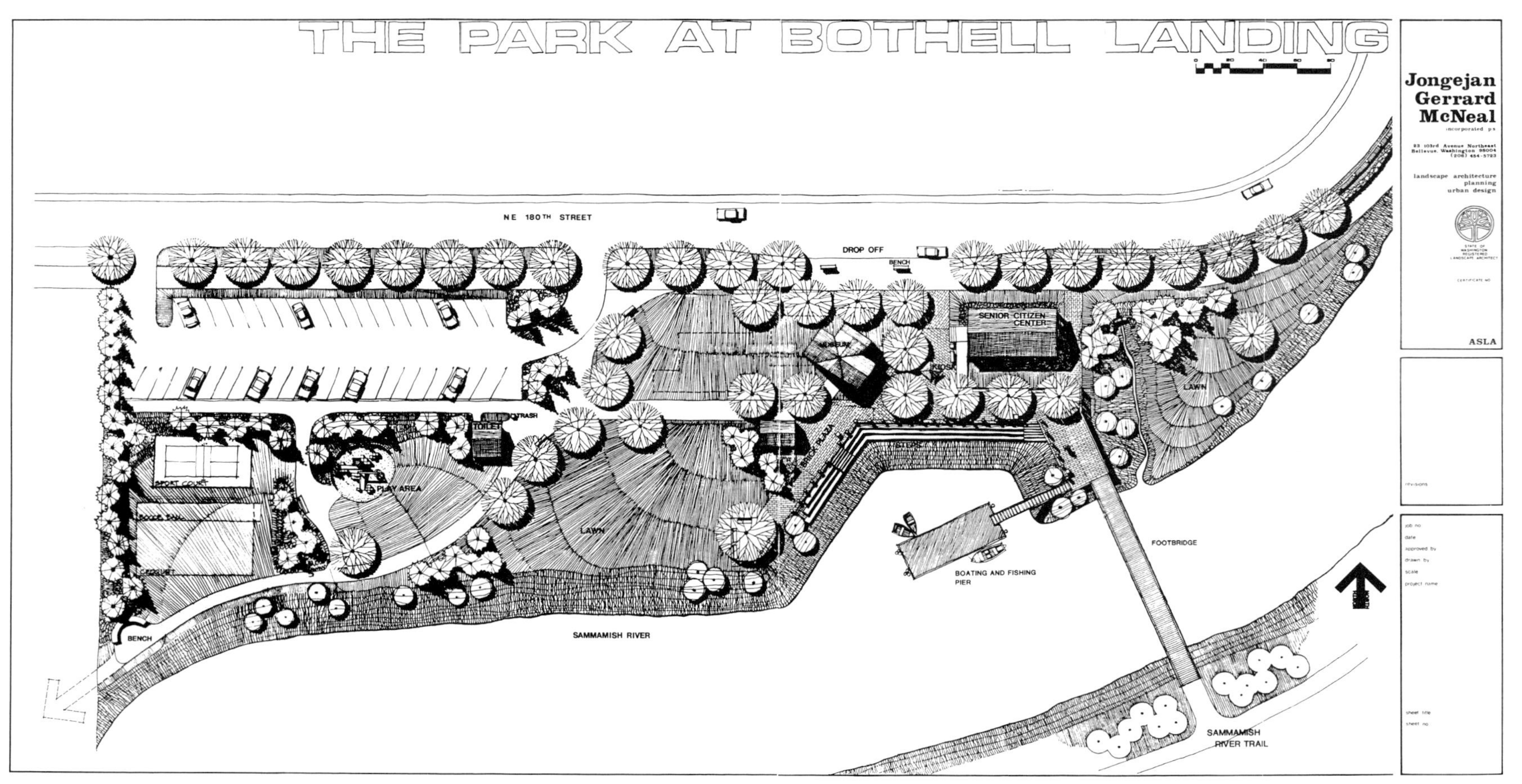

THE PARK AT BOTHELL LANDING
Jongejan Gerrard McNeal
incorporated ps
83 103rd Avenue Northeast
Bellevue, Washington 98004
(206) 454-5723
landscape architecture
planning
urban design
ASLA
NE 180TH STREET
DROP OFF
BENCH
SENIOR CITIZEN CENTER
LAWN
TRASH
TOILET
PLAY AREA
SPORT COURT
LAWN
BENCH
BOATING AND FISHING PIER
FOOTBRIDGE
SAMMAMISH RIVER
SAMMAMISH RIVER TRAIL

THE PARK AT BOTHELL LANDING
Bothell, Washington

Design firm: Jongejan/Gerrard/McNeal

This park site on the edge of the Sammamish River was originally a steamboat landing when the community was founded over a century ago. Steamboats made frequent trips between this and other communities, and Seattle. Railroads and paved highways eventually replaced the steamboat.

Like many waterways it was neglected for many years and abandoned to trash and blackberries. To rejuvenate the area three historical buildings were moved to the site, one of which is now a historical museum. The second serves as a senior citizen center and the third is Bothell's first schoolhouse, a log structure which looks much as it did when built.

The riverbank was cut to make an inlet 170 feet long to provide room for moorage of small boats. At the site of the old steamboat pier is a multi-purpose dock, used for fishing, temporary boat moorage, and as a stage for jazz concerts, public ceremonies and dramatic productions. Spectator seating is provided by a series of terraces on the bank which creates an amphitheater with the river as a back drop.

The footbridge connects the park to a trail system and access to several larger park systems. It also connects to a seven-mile pedestrian and bicycle corridor through Seattle.

Multi-purpose dock and stage with historic structures in the background.

Footbridge provides access to trails on both sides of the river.

Wood and brick terraces are spectator seating along the river bank.

Portion of hiking trail.

Timber supported drinking fountain.

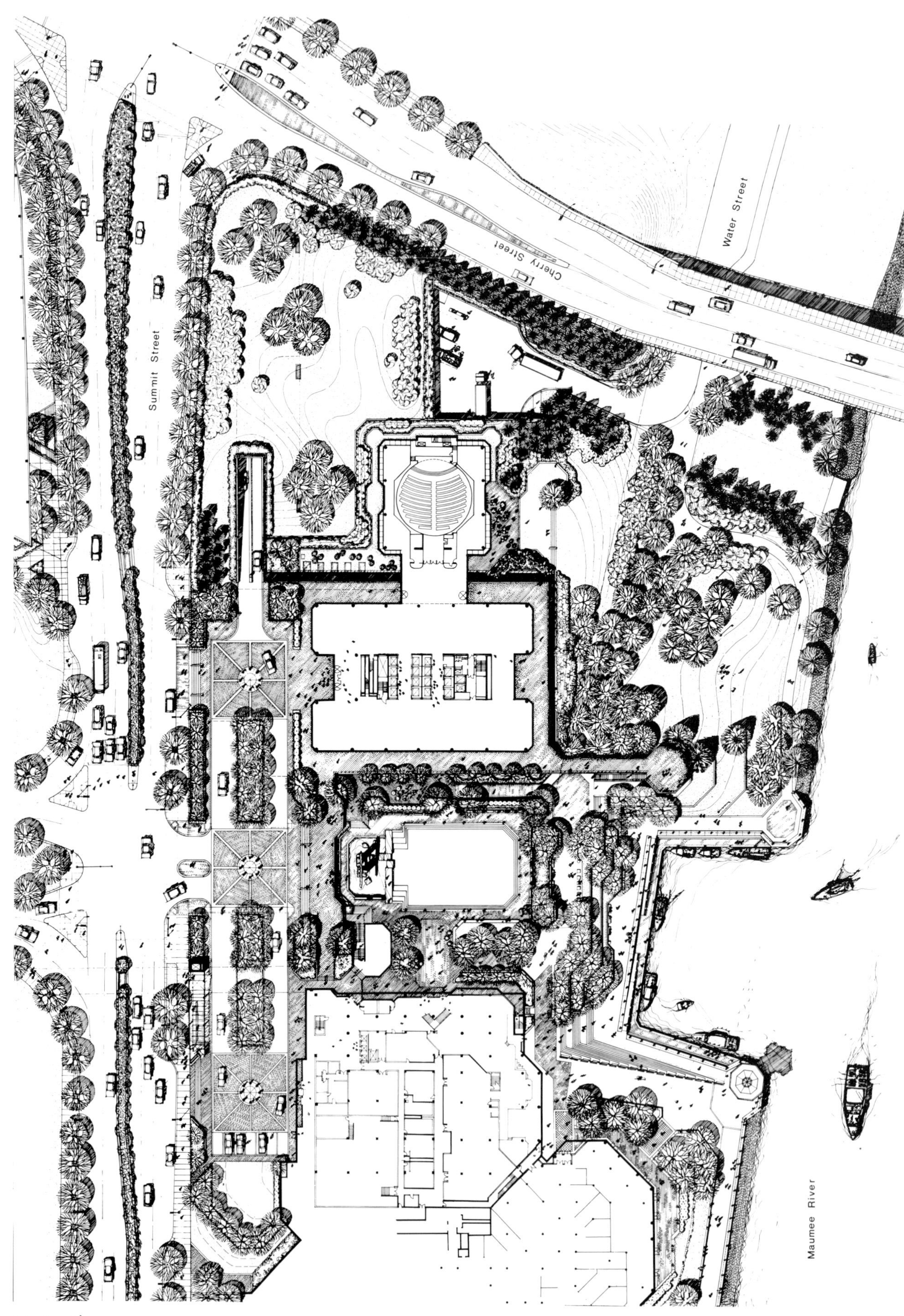

Master Plan.

PROMENADE PARK
Toledo, Ohio

Design firm: Sasaki Associates

Promenade Park integrates public and private developments into a continuous public open space along the Maumee riverfront. It revitalizes a deteriorated waterfront and allows a renewed pedestrian access to this area as well as encouraging redevelopment and improvement of adjacent areas. This 15-acre linear park includes river overlooks; an outdoor amphitheater oriented toward a water-edge stage; a lighthouse pavilion; open lawns, benches, and low walls for seating; and a boat basin accommodating pleasure craft and tour boats.

Because of the riverfront's difficult geotechnical conditions, the designers conducted extensive alternative analyses reflecting water level fluctuations, wind and wave energy, and ice forces. Based on cost and amenity design considerations, the river edge was improved with a combination of stone-clad revetments and sheet pile bulkheads. Park construction and river edge improvements incorporate major municipal utility systems which existed in the waterfront area.

Revitalized waterfront with river-edge stage.

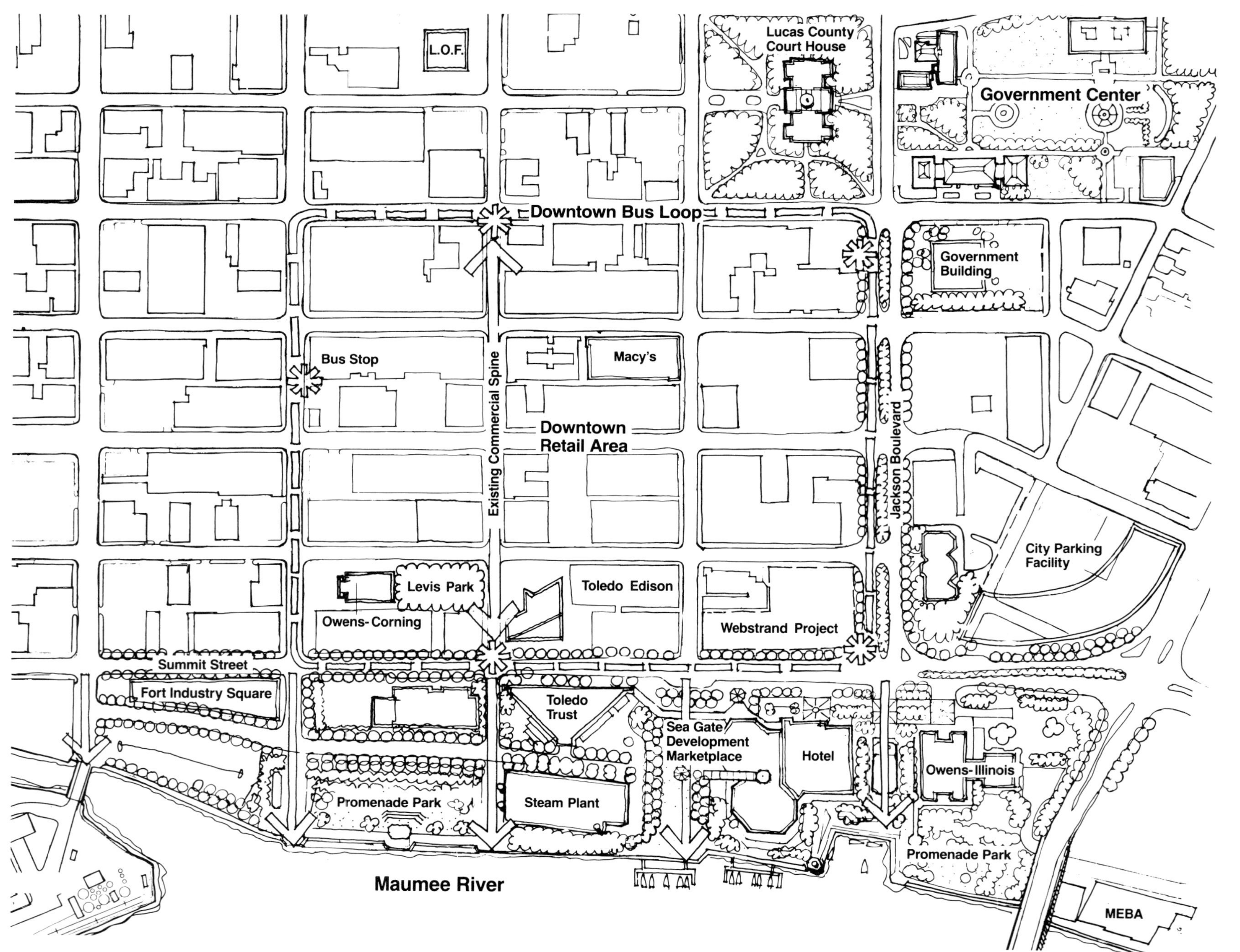

Promenade Park as it relates to downtown Toledo.

River, walkways, and amphitheatre.

Closeup of the serpentine wall. River-edge stage for activities on the Ohio River.

YEATMAN'S COVE, THE SERPENTINE WALL
Cincinnati, Ohio

Design firm: Zion and Breen Associates

The Serpentine Wall was conceived to provide pedestrian access to the Ohio River near downtown Cincinnati. It is very near the Riverfront Stadium. The wall provides aesthetic interest because of its shape. It is functional in that it provides seating for all kinds of river based activities. It is built to tolerate periodic flooding which is characteristic of the Ohio River and has become a monumental sculpture familiar to all the local citizenry.

Airview of the serpentine wall between two bridges over the Ohio River near Cincinnati's downtown.

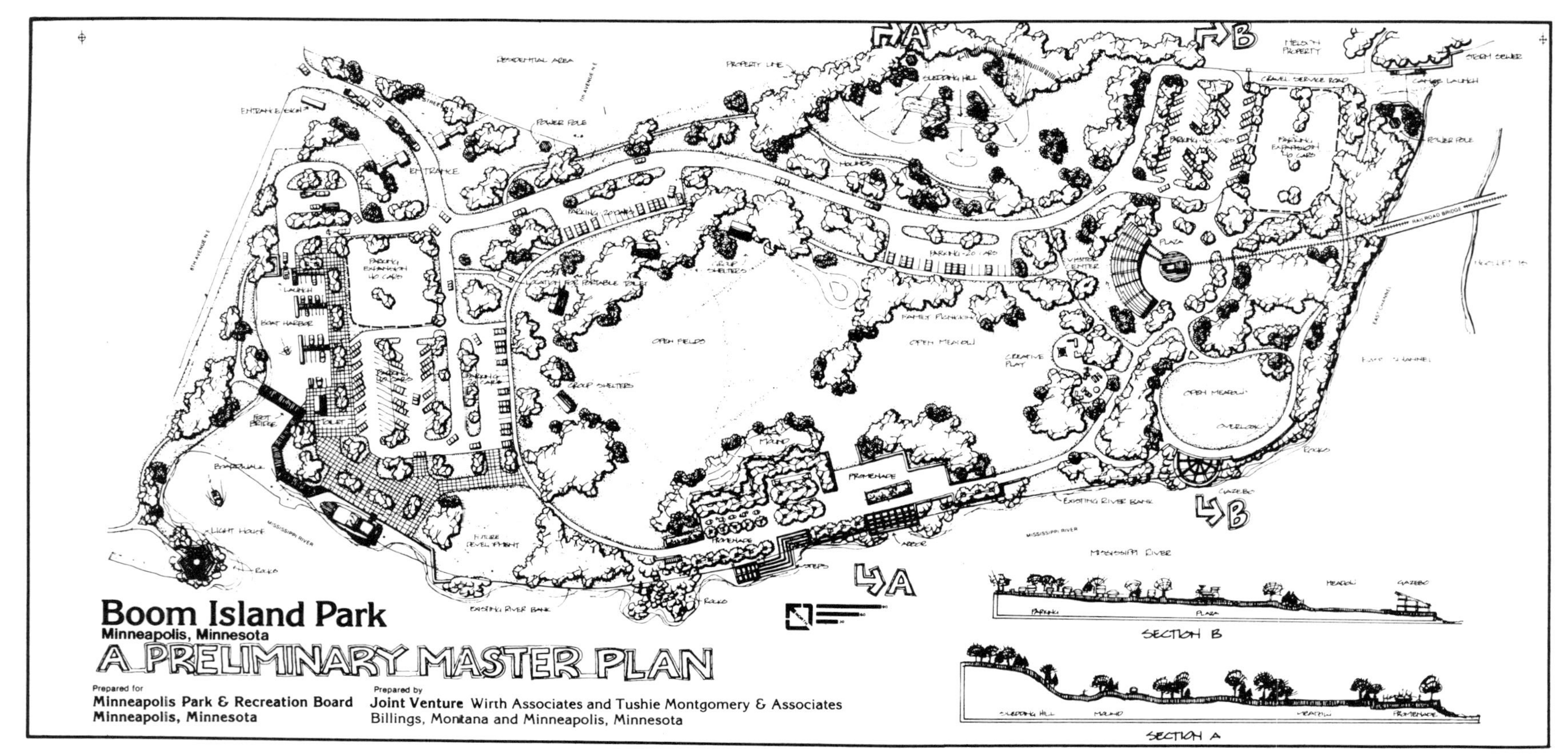

Boom Island Park
Minneapolis, Minnesota
A PRELIMINARY MASTER PLAN
Prepared for
Minneapolis Park & Recreation Board
Minneapolis, Minnesota
Prepared by
Joint Venture Wirth Associates and Tushie Montgomery & Associates
Billings, Montana and Minneapolis, Minnesota
SECTION B
SECTION A

BOOM ISLAND PARK
Minneapolis, Minnesota

Design firms: Wirth Design Associates
Tushie Montgomery Associates

This park is on a 25 acre landfill adjacent to the Mississippi River in downtown Minneapolis. It is a part of an extensive, long-range, riverfront rehabilitation program and represents the first major development that front on and interfaces with the river. The park is also adjacent to a mixed ethnic neighborhood where second and third generations continue the strong traditions of their forefathers. They exerted a strong influence in the design of the park.

Orientation and access to the river, diversity of use to serve the entire community including the adjacent neighborhood were the underlying themes of the design effort. It was important that every user or group regardless of age or interest feel comfortable. Groups can celebrate their heritage close to the river with a view towards the city. A pedestrian can feel free to walk close to the water and even stick in his toes. There is space that a fisherman can call his own. Boaters can reach the water without a hassle. There is diversity of uses and activities for all ages and all seasons.

Each side of the river as it passes through Minneapolis is bordered by steep banks or industrialized development. At one time, Boom Island was an industrial site, but it differs from other properties bordering the river in that it is less than 12 feet above the river.

Boom Island is situated on a stretch of the Mississippi River immediately upstream from St. Anthony Falls and Nicollet Island where the city got its start. Because of the falls, the flow is slow enough to accommodate boating ranging from cruisers to canoes. Locks around the falls provide access to the entire length of the river. A combination boat basin and docking area was located close to the park entrance for easy access by traffic and boat trailers without penetrating the other parts of the park.

The promenade was purposely recessed 5 feet to provide closer association with the river and passive recreation. In addition it was surrounded with earth mounds to create a sense of isolation and separation from the activities of the group and family picnic areas.

The area at the southwest corner of the park is designed for viewing the river and the city skyline. Neighborhood groups can celebrate their special occasions here. An adjacent visitor's center serves both as an interpretive center and restroom facility as well as a terminal for a proposed trolley system that will connect the park to other river developments. The visitor center is designed as a replica of a railroad round house that once stood near the site when Boom Island served as a railroad yard near the turn of the century.

Group and family picnic areas with associated open space occupy the balance of the park. There is a sledding hill on an existing high bank along the east edge of the park for seasonal diversity.

Since the site had been a landfill excavation it revealed everything from sawdust to old bricks. These conditions required replacement and special compaction for foundations and special designs of pilings for the bulkheads along the river's edge.

Designer's concepts for boat harbor and Promenade at Boom Island Park.

Trolley terminal and group activity area.

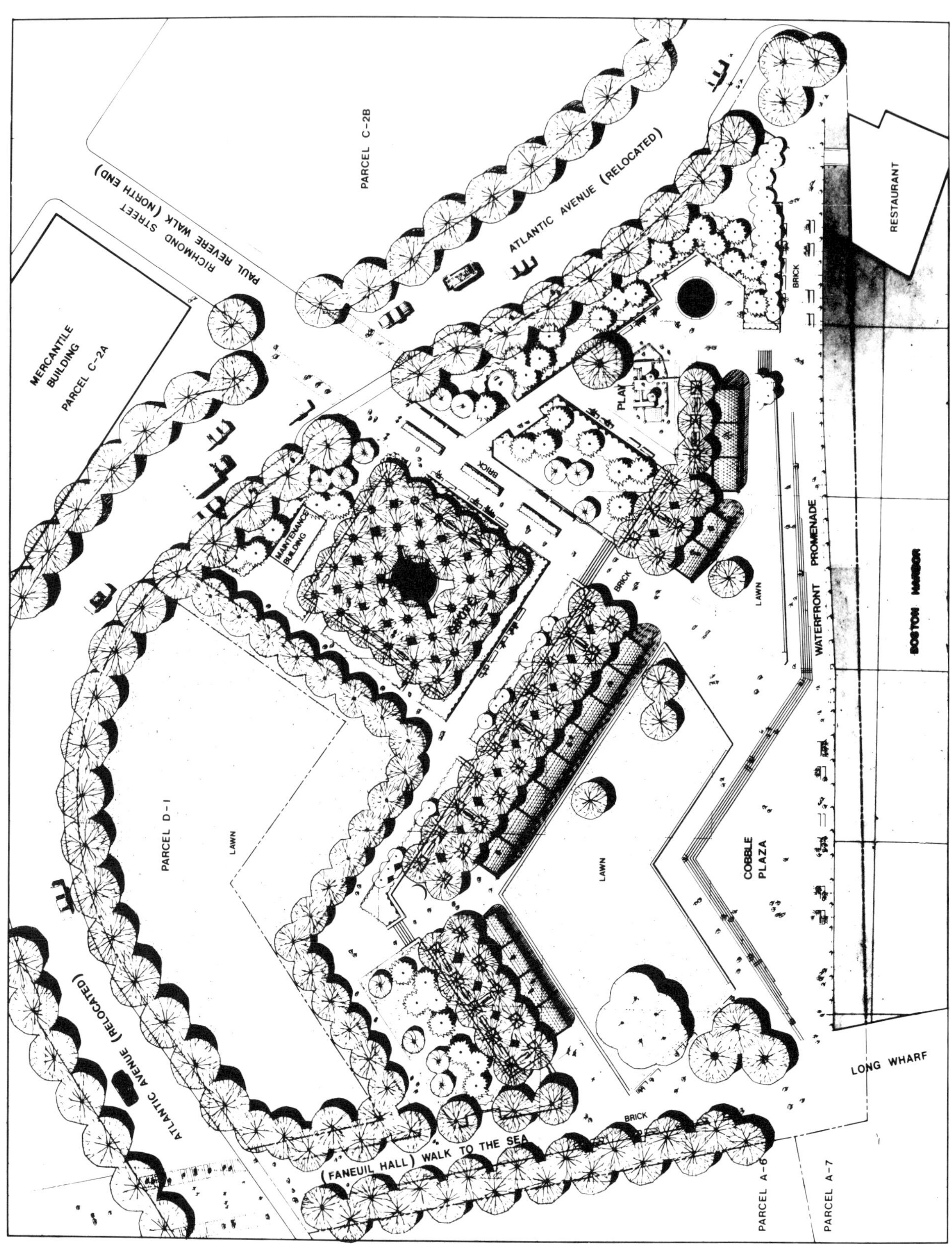

Master Plan for Waterfront Park.

WATERFRONT PARK
Boston, Massachusetts

Design firm: Sasaki Associates

This 4 1/2-acre waterfront park completes the pedestrian open space link from Boston's Government Center through the Faneuil Hall/Quincy Market area to the Harbor. The park also provides a link from the waterfront along Richmond Street to the Paul Revere house.

The design accommodates the passive recreational activities of adults and children in a series of small park spaces. A grove of honey locust trees focuses on a decorative fountain. The stone dust finish of the grove area was selected as an appropriate surface for bocci and other informal games. A timber play sculpture resembling a shipwreck provides for more strenuous activities in a nearby space. The park's main plaza is surrounded by sloped lawns oriented toward the harbor and is designed to accommodate exhibits, theatrical productions, or seaside concerts. A wood trellis defines this plaza and connects the park subareas. The existing granite bulkhead was restored and capped with a granite header. Cast iron bollards and chain delineate the water edge.

The materials used in the park reflect its historic setting and oceanfront exposure. The brick walkways and the reuse of cobblestone street material harmonize with building and site materials in adjacent areas. Plant materials were selected for their ability to thrive in a saltwater environment.

Edge of the waterfront at Boston Harbor. Park is to the right.

Trellis is the central visual theme and ties the park together.

Seating under the trellis.

Play structure resembling a shipwreak.

Walkway and Amphitheatre. Photos by Tom Vageline.

Picnic shelter.

SOUTH POINTE PARK
Miami Beach, Florida

Design firm: Post, Buckley, Schuh & Jernigan

This park is situated on the southern tip of Miami Beach where it is surrounded on three sides by water, one side of which is the Atlantic Ocean. It is designed for multi-use passive and active recreational functions. It also serves as the site for city festivals and cultural activities. Some of the facilities include an amphitheatre with covered stage and adjacent dressing rooms, boardwalk systems, observation towers, picnic shelters, and a fitness trail system. One of the last original sand dunes in the area is on this site. It has been reconstructed and replanted with specially selected native dune species.

Amphitheatre.

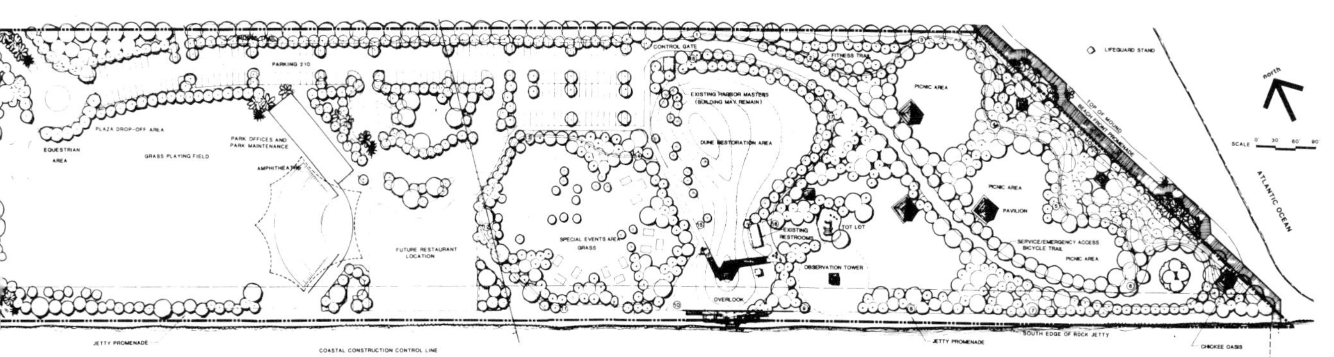

Observation tower and play area.

LANDFILL PARK
Broward County, Florida

Design firm: Post, Buckley, Schuh & Jernigan

Since 1980, Broward County has been expanding in population as one the of the fastest growing counties in the United States. All of South Florida is experiencing the same rapid growth. A by-product of this growth is the increased need for public services of all kinds including the disposal of municipal wastes. Some areas are using recycling programs to reduce the disposable waste and others are burning the flammable fractions to generate electricity. The problem is to dispose of large volumes of waste in the most environmentally safe and cost effective way.

Broward County chose to reduce waste volume by incineration and generate electricity to create revenue. Because of the time lag in getting a plant in operation, an interim contingency landfill was required. It would also be needed to handle construction debris, tree and shrub trimmings, etc., as well as all waste during a recovery plant breakdown.

The rate of waste accumulation at the landfill would be large at first until the recovery plant was built and in operation after which it would be greatly reduced. In the first 1-1/2 years of operation 100 acres would be used until the recovery plant was in operation. After that approximately 40 acres would be used in each 5 year period.

The goal of the County was to not only solve the waste disposal problem but protect the Biscayne Aquifer which lies below the county and serves as its principal source of potable water. It also wanted to convert this facility into a regional park at the conclusion of the landfill process. However, it was estimated that is would be 40 years before the landfill process was completed and that was too long for the site to be unusable. Therefore, it became desirable to convert portions of the landfill to park use soon after they became closed.

It was determined that a buffer was needed between the landfill and adjacent residential areas, so the first 40 acres at the northeast corner was immediately designated for park use and not included in the land to be used for landfill. Between the park and landfill a canal and lake system would be developed to act as a moat to prevent people from crossing from the park into the landfill.

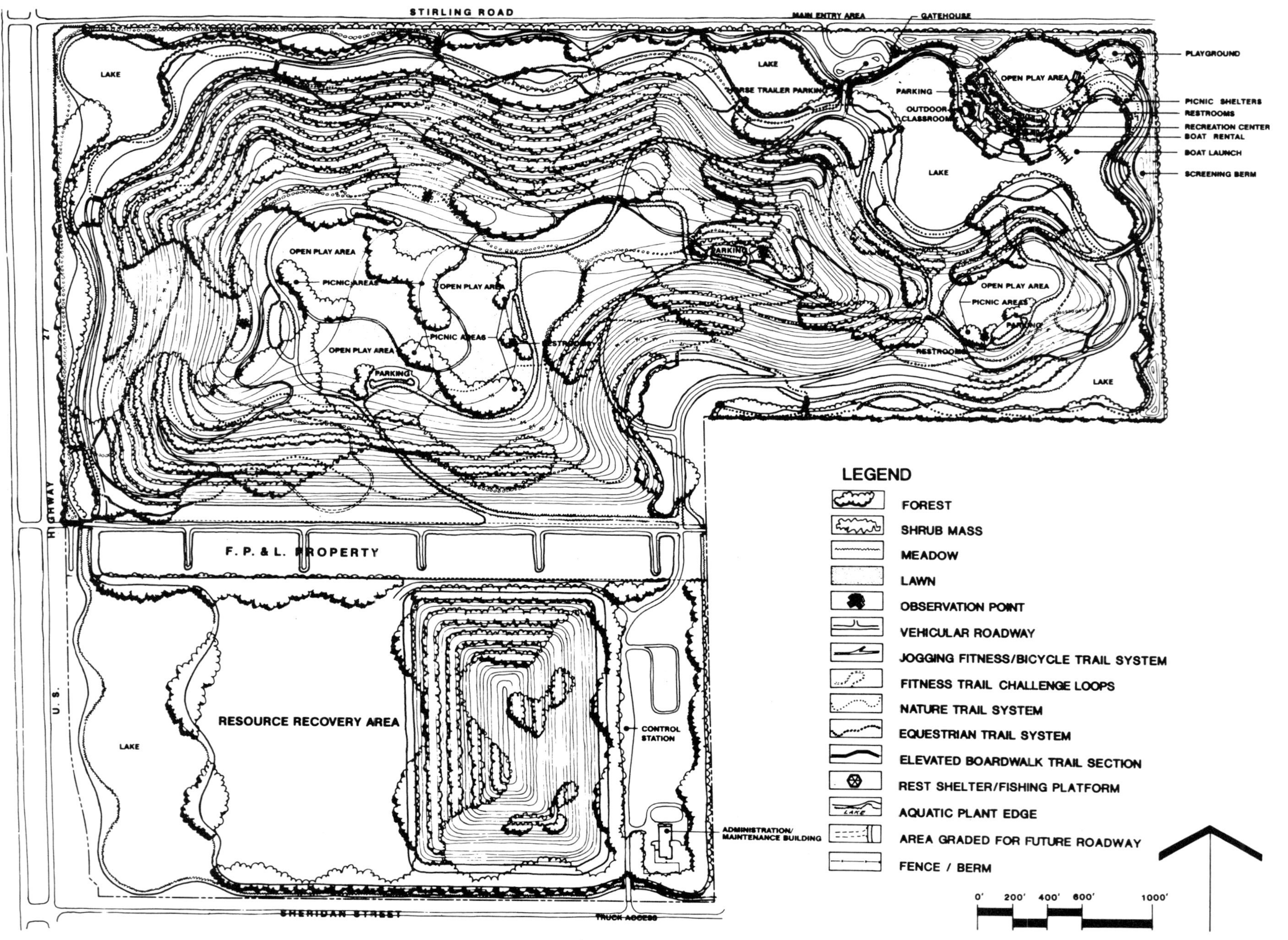

Master Plan for Landfill Park.

The remainder of the site was designed to reach an ultimate height of 125 feet. The landfill was to be engineered so that the final mounding would be curvilinear in shape and have predesignated high points and views that could be used for future park purposes. In flat Florida such a park would be very dramatic. The views across the surrounding countryside would be spectacular.

Staging the construction of the landfill was a challenge to minimize litter, odors, vermin and noise. Starting at the northeast and moving west reduced the impact of breeze and wind movements. Additional separation was arranged by placing the access roads for the landfill and park a mile apart from each other. Park visitors are not in contact with waste hauling vehicles. The landfill mound would buffer landfill equipment such as bulldozers, compactors, trucks, etc. Noise would be deflected to the west away from the park and residential areas.

Initially it was proposed that the landfill be only 55 feet in height, but since the ultimate use of this site is for park uses and not landfill, the shape of the fill had to be modified so that the capacity of the site would not be diminished, while providing land forms for an effective and meaningful park facility. Some of the plateaus which will serve as open play areas for football, softball, and so forth, will be at 37 and 98 feet in height. The contouring of the landform is done in such a way as to create large curving hillside areas and to give the impression of a naturalistic shape to the overall site. The surface water retention area at the base of the landform will also have a curvilinear and meandering character to complement both the landform, the canal and lake system created in the initial park development at the northeast corner. This park is intended to become a major naturalistic, wildlife habitat, native planting, active and passive regional recreational facility.

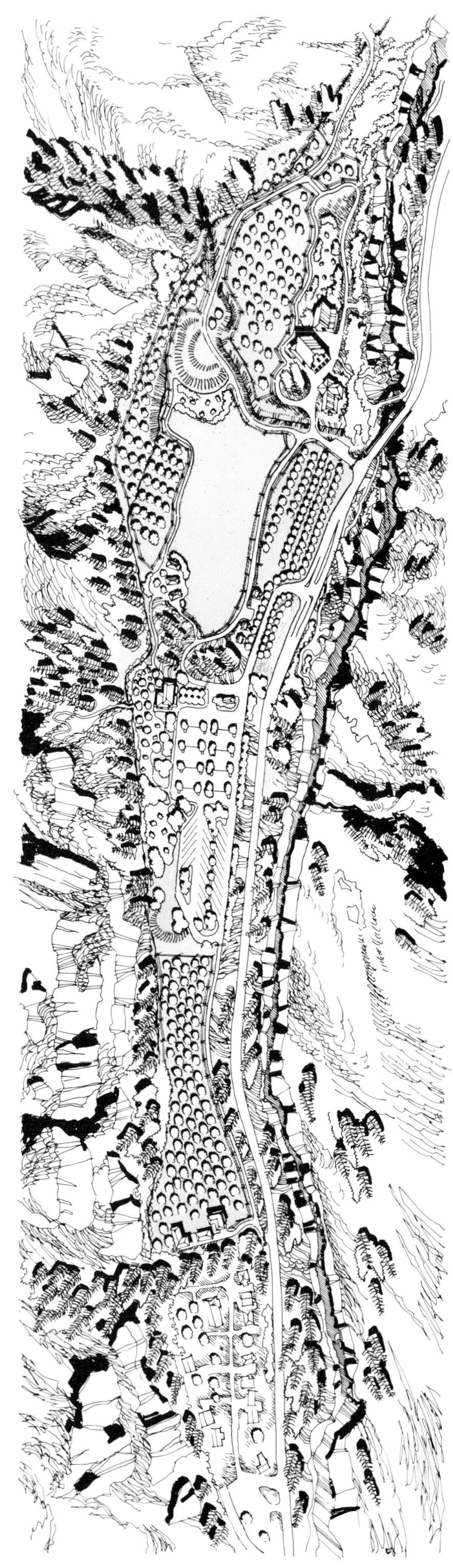

Master Plan for Slide Rock State Park.

SLIDE ROCK STATE PARK
Sedona, Arizona

Design firm: EDAW, Inc.

A few miles north of Sedona in Oak Creek Canyon is a popular natural water recreation site known as "Slide Rock." The flow of water over grooved smooth rock and the beauty of the canyon attracts thousands of visitors each year. A 43-acre area adjacent to Slide Rock has been acquired in order to provide adequate parking and other necessary facilities to support this unique recreation resource.

Natural slide feature of Oak Creek which gives the park its name.

Lower section of the natural slide area.

Some of the natural beauty of the park area.

The site is colorful with green foliage contrasting against red and salmon tinted rock.

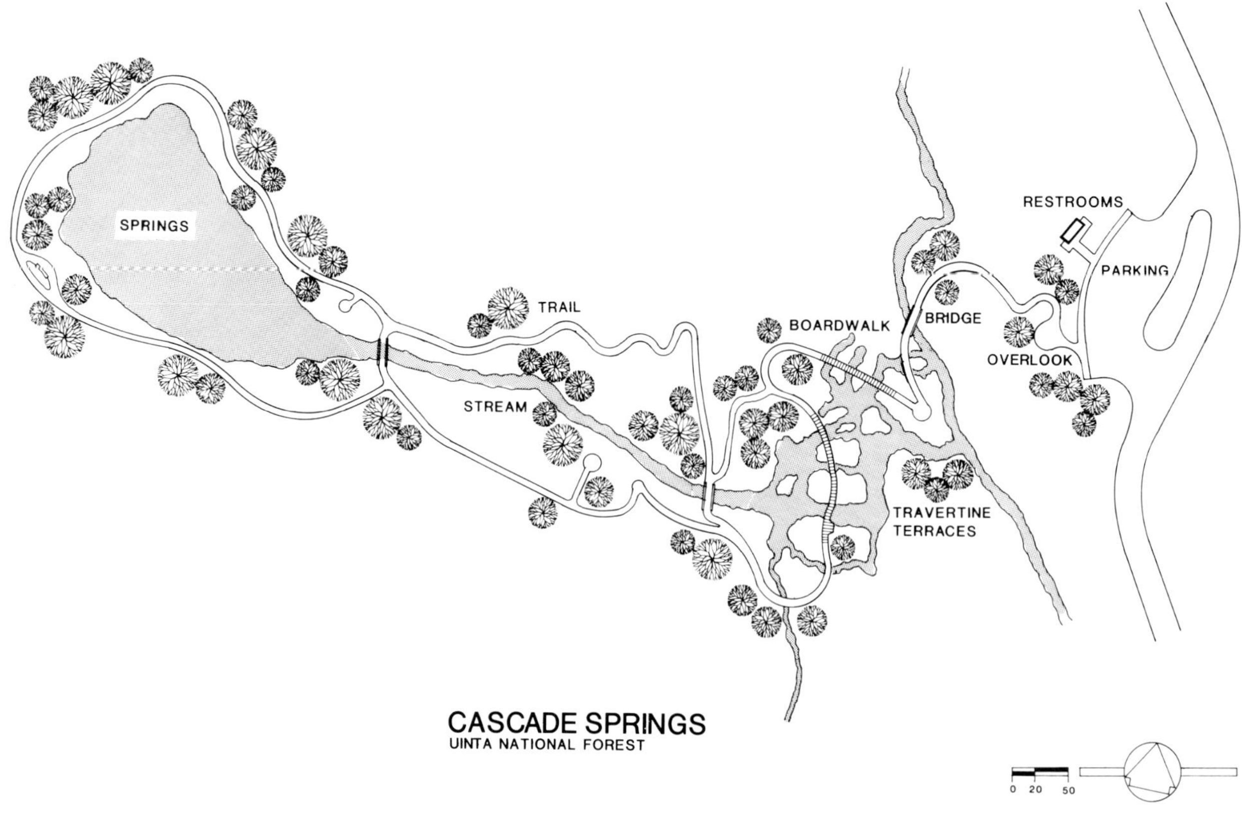

CASCADE SPRINGS
UINTA NATIONAL FOREST

CASCADE SPRINGS
Uintah National Forest, Utah

Design firm: U.S. Forest Service

High in the mountains northeast of Provo, Utah is a scenic area where spring water oozes from the ground. The water over a large area merges into a stream which runs to a lower elevation where it fans out and cascades over a series of travertine terraces. The terraces were formed over several centuries from limestone eaten away by the spring water somewhere deep within the earth and then redeposited along the terraces. The waterfalls or cascades offer spectacular beauty and access to them has been provided with paths and boardwalks. Visitors can get close to the cascading water, floating watercress and wildflowers.

On the left water cascades over a travertine terrace almost hidden by yellow wildflowers and watercress.

Bridge over the stream which connects the springs to the travertine terraces to the right.

A portion of the boardwalk that winds through a bed of watercress between travertine terraces.

One of several signs in the park which describes for the visitor the natural phenomena they are viewing.

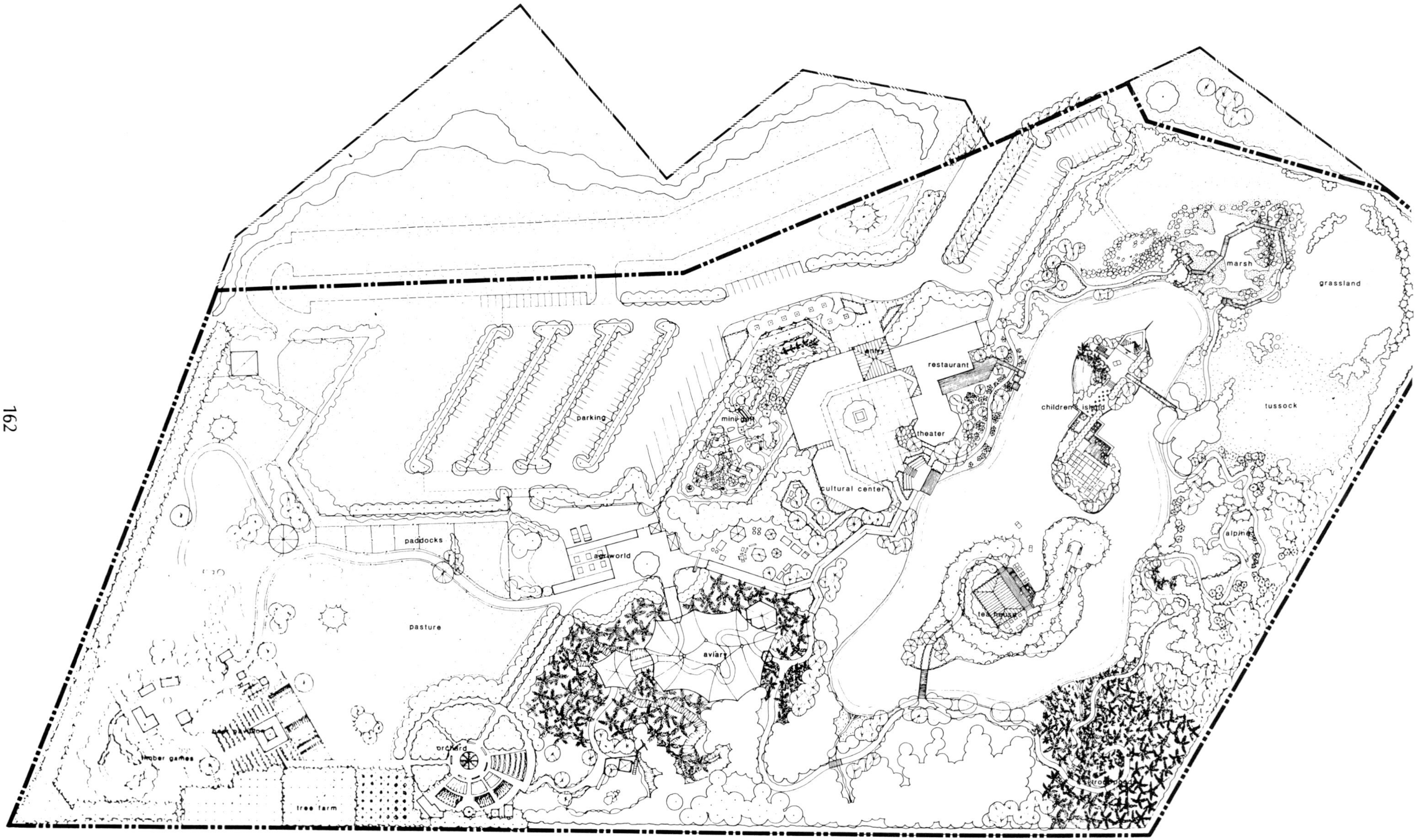

MASTER PLAN

NEW ZEALAND HERITAGE PARK

NEW ZEALAND HERITAGE PARK
Auckland, New Zealand

Design firms: EDAW, Inc.
Mogal/Beckett Sterling

     Located on a 22 acre former quarry site in Auckland, the park includes exhibits, demonstrations and participatory activities featuring New Zealand's cultural history, native flora and fauna and agricultural activities. Much of the cultural history is presented through audio-visual techniques in a special cultural center building. Other buildings include a major entry pavilion featuring exclusively New Zealand projects, an agricenter for farm-related demonstrations, a walk-in aviary, a noctural house and a small animal house.

     An on-site water source is being used to create a display of the famous New Zealand trout. The water also supplies a 3-acre lake which serves both as a visual and recreational attraction. Within the lake are play islands, one each for children and adults, where culturally based amusement activities are located.

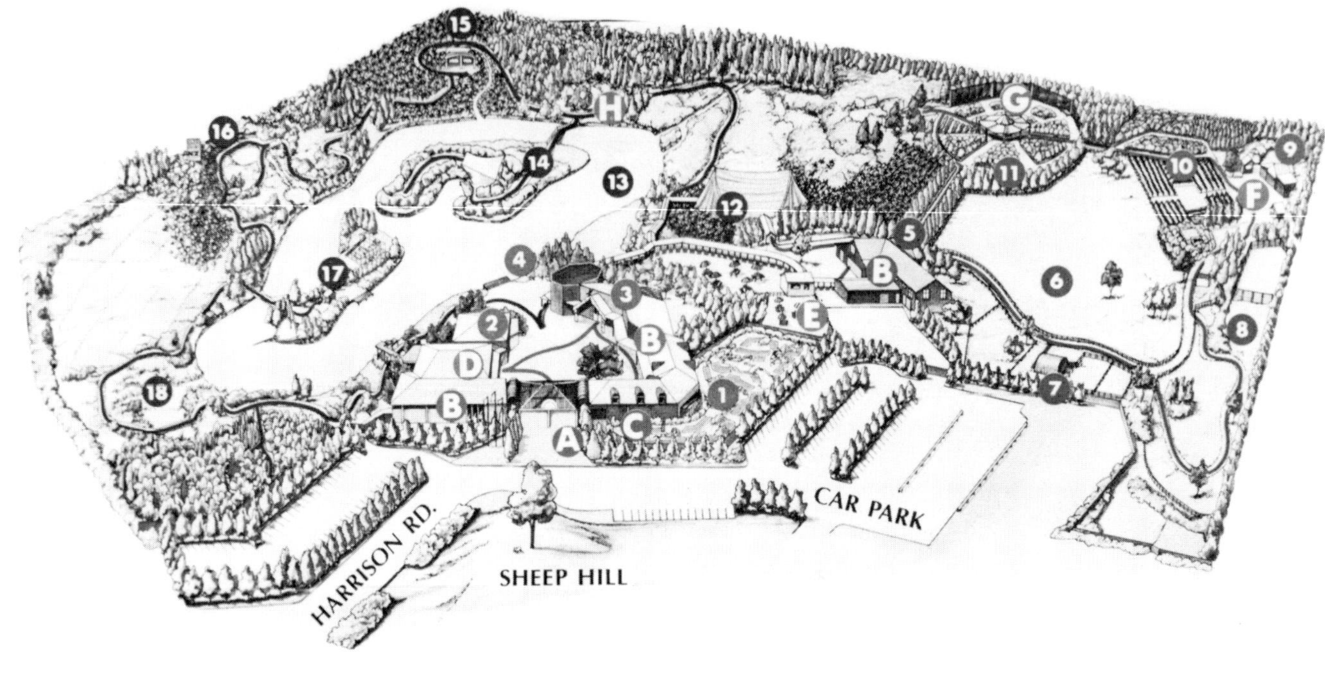

A. Visitor Information
B. Restrooms
C. New Zealand Product Shop and Park Exit
D. Aotearoa Restaurant and Bar
E. BBQ Snack Bar
F. Kauri Kitchen
G. Pavlova Paradise

1. Mini Golf
2. Tasman Theatre
3. Cultureworld
4. Boat Dock
5. The Barn
6. Farm Animals
7. Animal Petting
8. Top Paddock: Deer
9. Timberland, Sawmill
10. Vineyard
11. Orchard
12. Kiwi House and Freelight Aviary
13. Lake Heritage
14. Hibiscus Haven
15. Trout Pools
16. Alpine Hill
17. Moa Island Playground

Educational signage in park.

Concept sketch of park entrance.

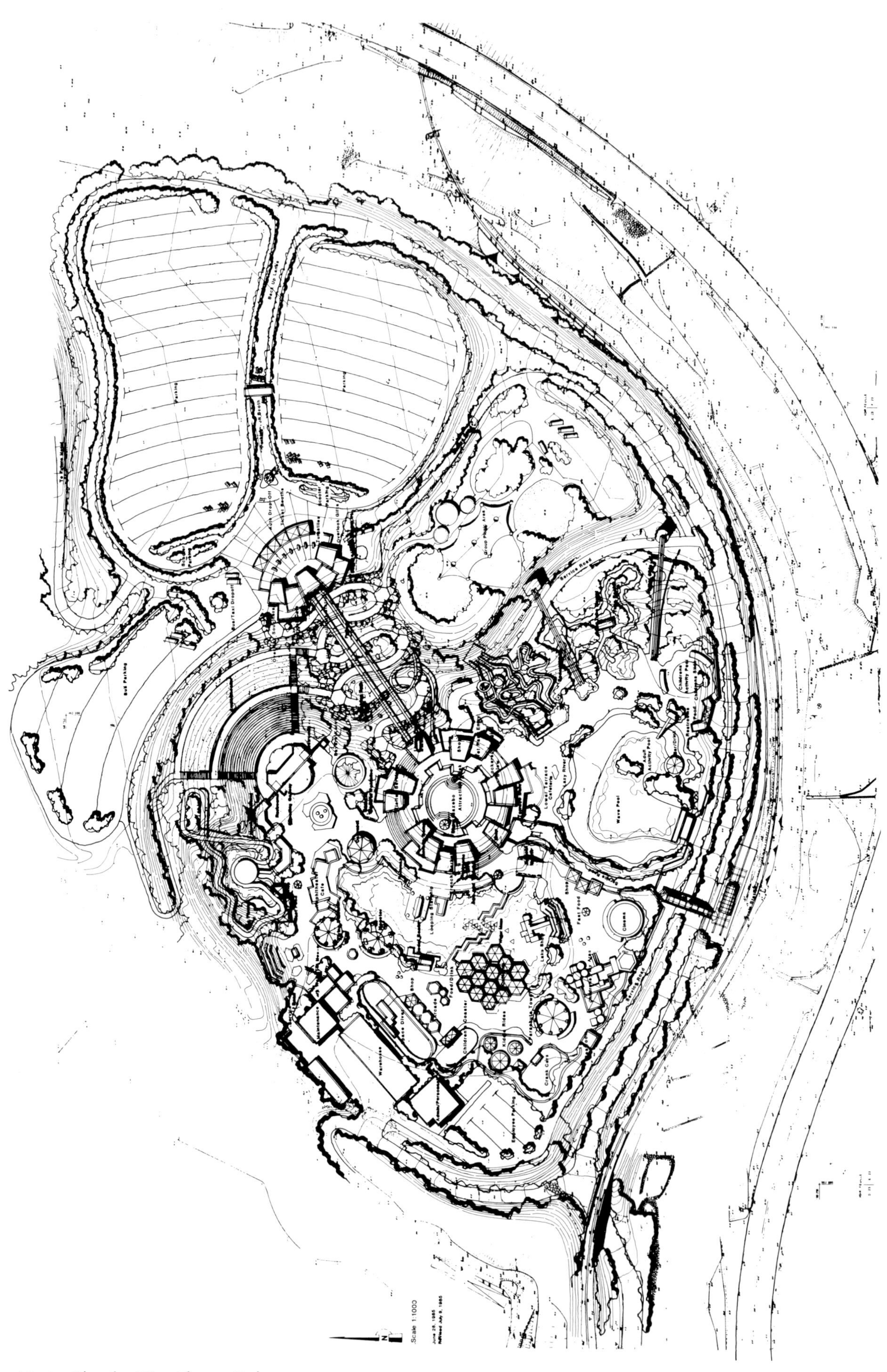

Master Plan for Nice Theme Park.

166

NICE THEME PARK
Nice, France

Design firm: EDAW, Inc.

A unique theme amusement park in the Cote d'Azur region of France. Water park and amusement-type rides, attractions and show facilities are included surrounding a central core of restaurants, shops and other visitor uses. Humorous and unusual themes are developed throughout, emphasizing fantasy, imagination and the absurd. The site covers 34 hectares which had been previously quarried for Nice Airport expansion, thus significant topographic change makes a dramatic park setting. Funicular access links the main parking area above with the central plaza. Several French engineers and architects collaborated with the design firm on this project. The feasibility analysis was performed by Economics Research Associates.

Concept sketch for Theme Park.

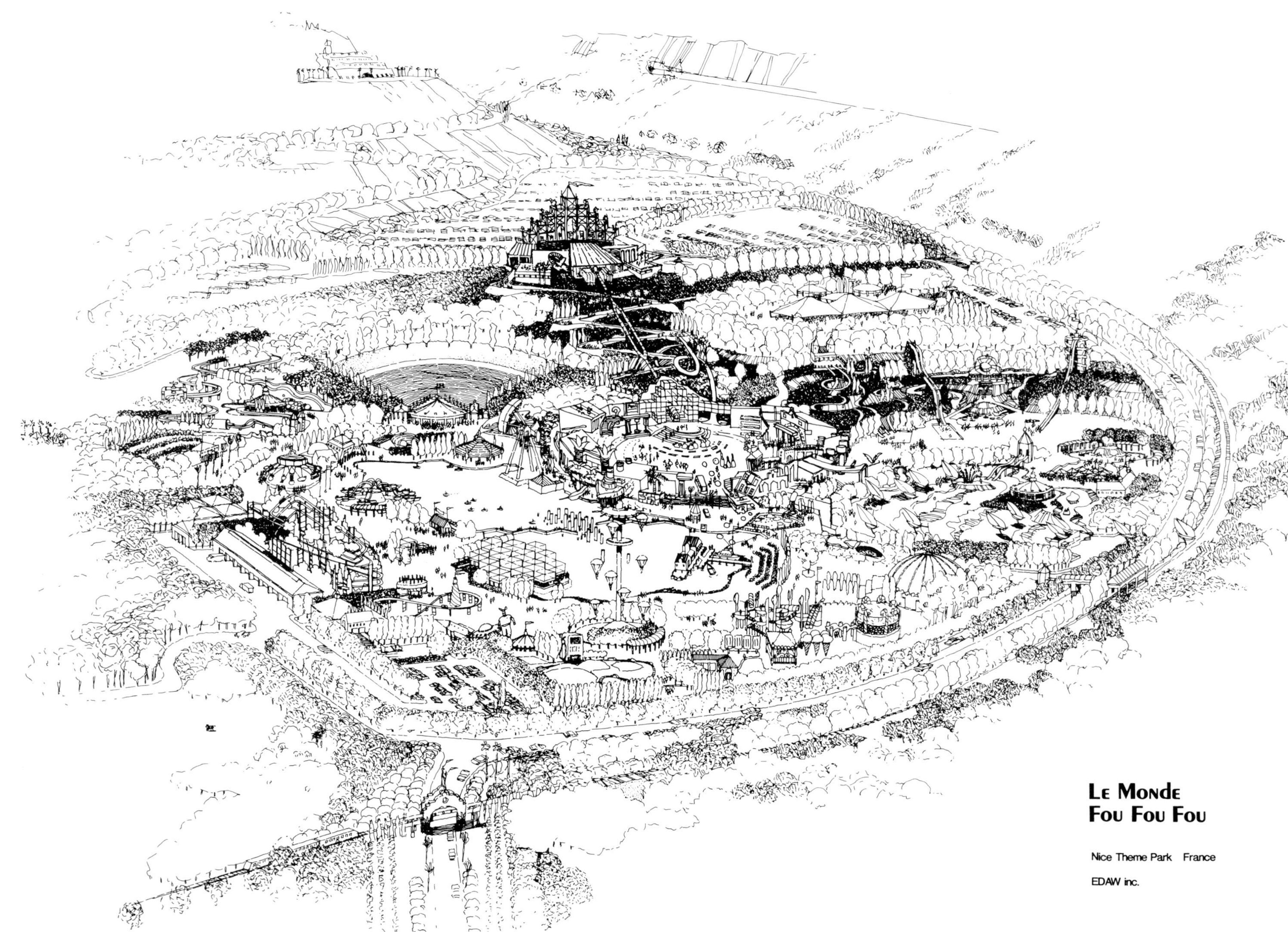

Le Monde
Fou Fou Fou

Nice Theme Park   France

EDAW inc.

ASIR NATIONAL PARK
Saudi Arabia

Design firms: Wirth/Berger
Idea Center
Consortium West

Asir National Park is located in the southwestern corner of Saudi Arabia. It is 644 kilometers south of the holy city of Mecca, less than 200 kilometers across the Red Sea from Ethiopia, and 70 kilometers north of North Yemen. Within its boundaries are some of the more scenic areas of the Asir-Tehama region, but excluded are lands which are heavily populated and under cultivation.

The scenic areas range from the white sand beaches and coral reefs of the Red Sea to the soaring cliffs of the great Arabian escarpment, some of which are as imposing as the one wall of the Grand Canyon in the United States.

A modern highway follows the ancient caravan trails with their many switchbacks. It passes fallen sentinel towers as it reaches the 1800 meter plateau where cool breezes lift wisping clouds against the walls of the escarpment. Africans, Muslems, Bedouins, Yemeni and Saudi Arabians share the park land. There is a distinct presence of age, man and nature.

The park was established to conserve for the people of Saudi Arabia an outstanding example of their natural and cultural heritage. This is characterized by the Great Rift, its geology, flora, fauna, and cultural history. The purpose of the park is to provide protection for the region's resources and leave them unimpaired for the benefit of future generations.

The scenic splendor of the steep terrain is the result of faulting, massive uplifts, volcanism and erosion. The park's 455 hectares span five distinct ecological areas: the seashore, tehama, foothills, escarpment, plateau and mountains. The park rises from the Red Sea to over 3048 meters with a narrow band 160-240 kilometers wide. During the summer days when the rest of Saudi Arabia swelters in 49 degree Centrigrade days and nights, the park areas reach 29 degree C and cools to 15 degree C at night. Vegetation within the park is influenced by climate, soil, topography, drainage and water supply. From the sands of the seashore to the peaks of Jabal Al Sawdah, the plant life is the most diverse and abundant in the Kingdom. The park is "home" to species existing nowhere else in Saudi Arabia.

The mammals, large and small birds and reptiles are similar to those in East Africa. Occasionally leopards are seen as well as hyena, baboons jackals, wolves and fox. There are 300 different bird species including the large and endangered species, lammergeier. Reptiles include skinks, scaly lizards, chameleons and green tree frogs. There are also vipers, puff adders, and Egyptian cobras.

Facilities have been placed at several locations throughout the park and include a visitor interpretive/information center, park headquarters, camping, picnicking, overlooks, beach and bathing areas.

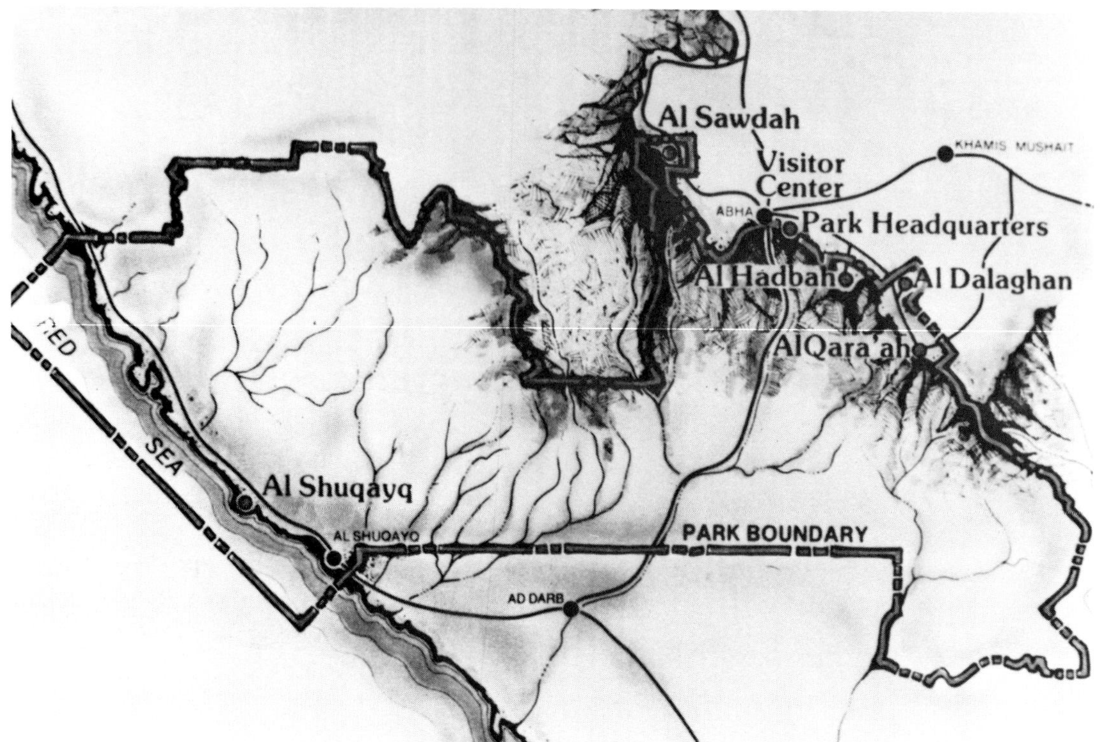

Boundary and location map of Asir National Park in southwest Saudi Arabia.

Sketch of park terrain.

Concept sketch of visitor's center.

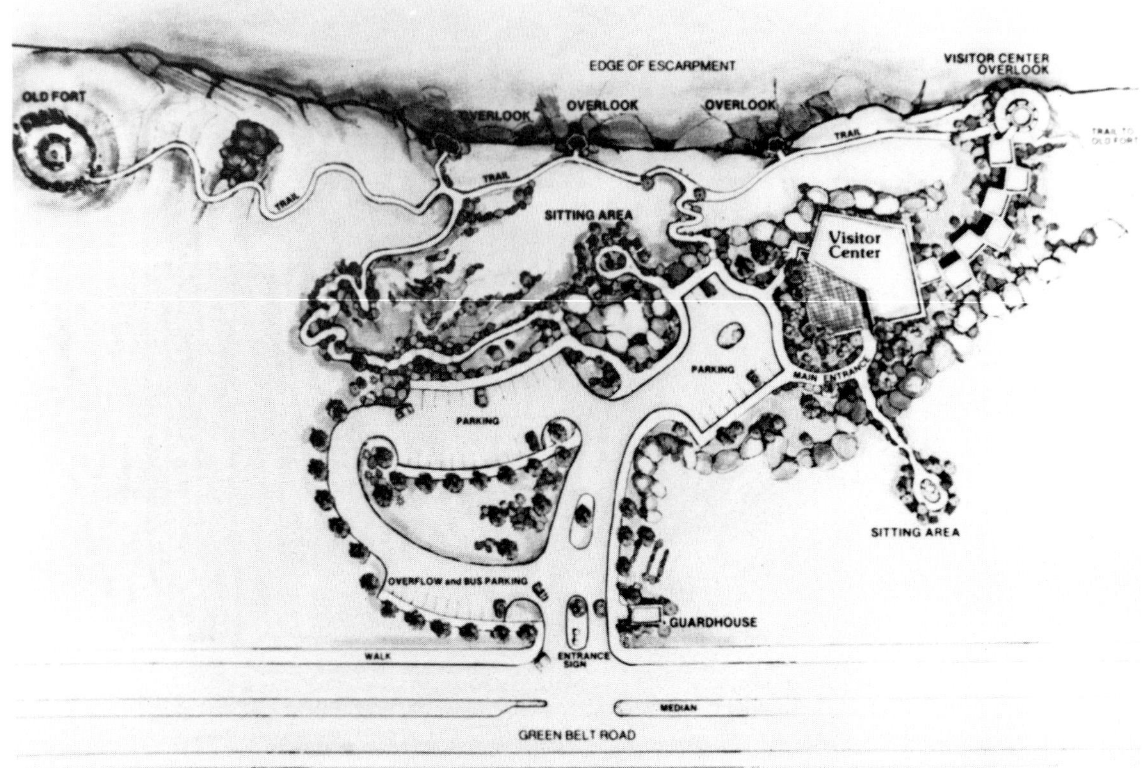

Site plan for visitor's center.

Concept sketch for play area.

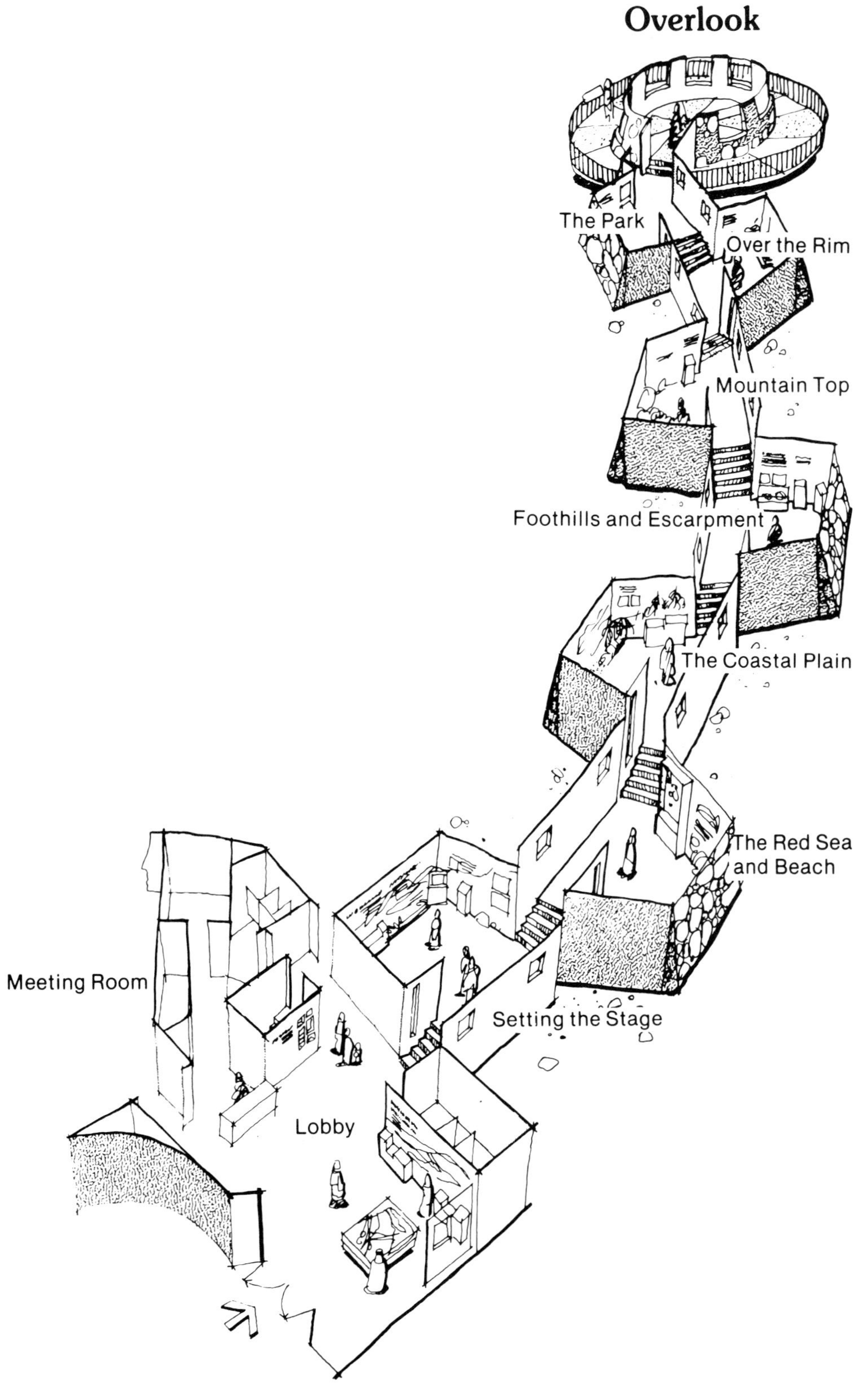

Layout of visitor's center.

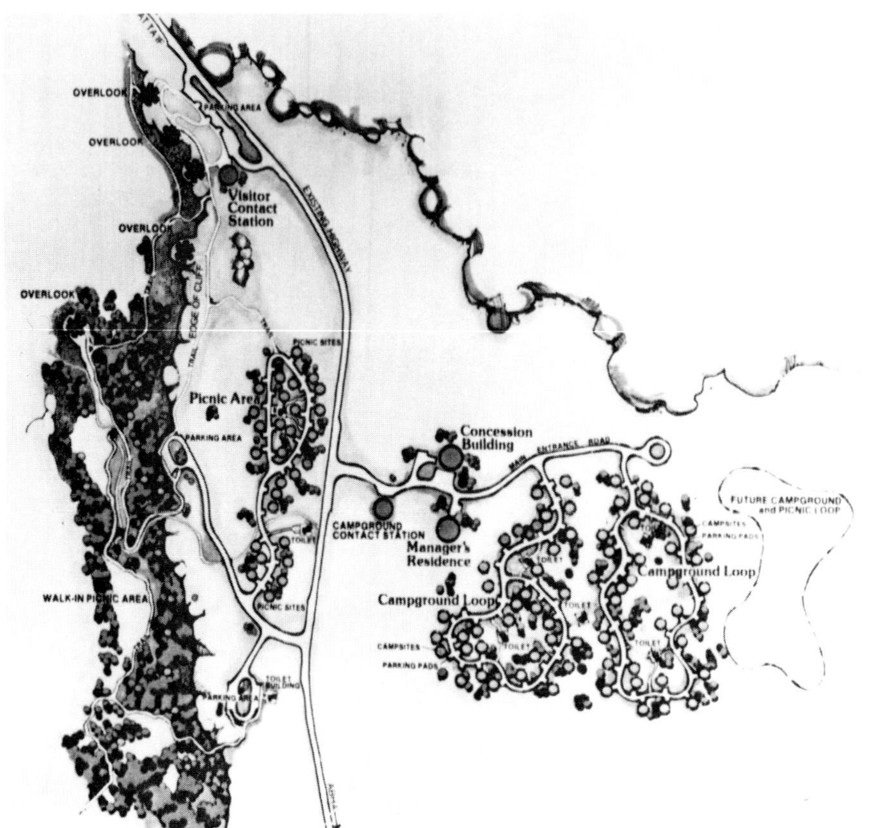

Site plan for typical campground.

Concept sketch for picnic shelter.

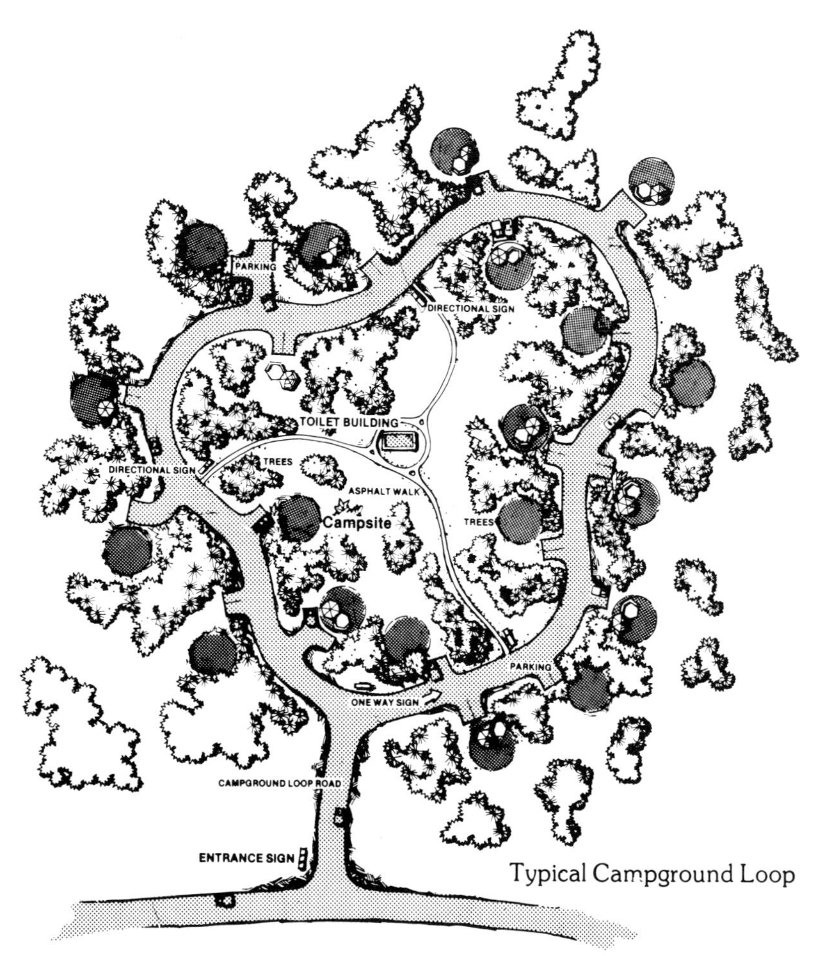

Typical Campground Loop

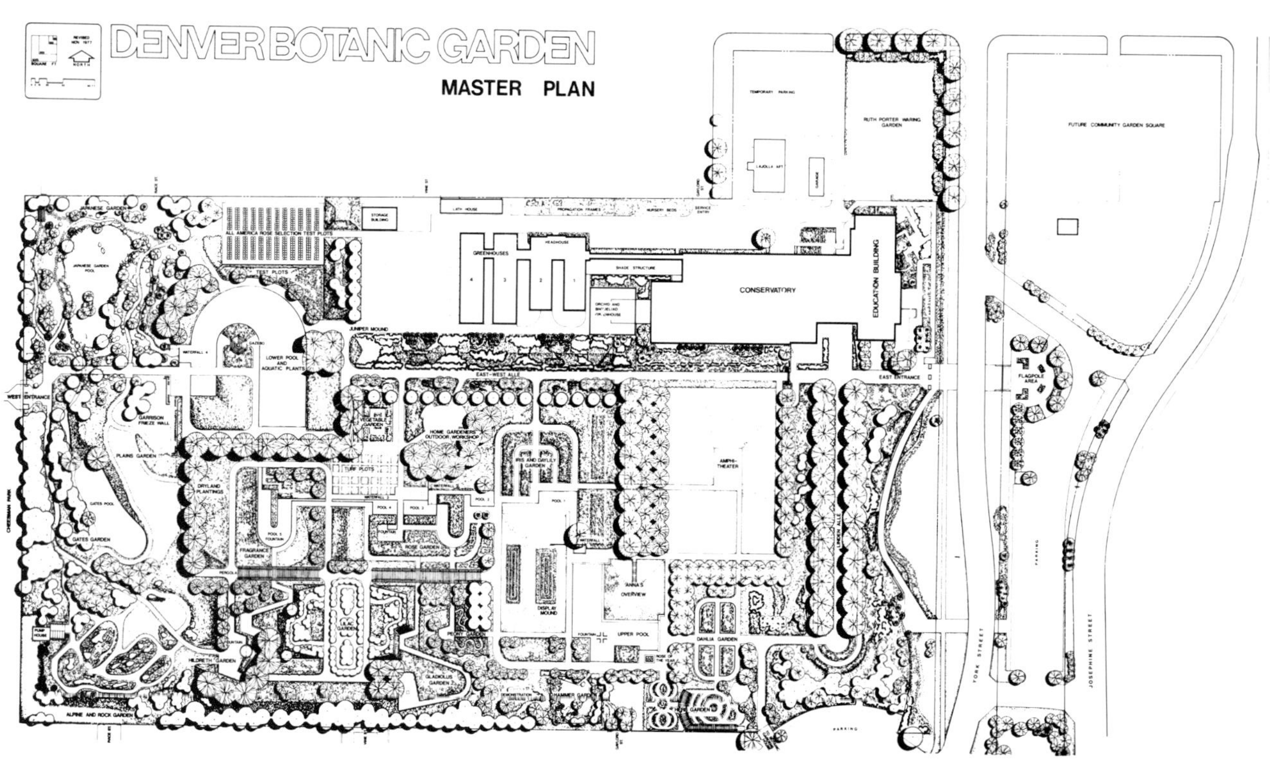

DENVER BOTANIC GARDEN
MASTER PLAN

DENVER BOTANIC GARDENS
Denver, Colorado

Design firm: EDAW, Inc.

The Gardens are located on a 20-acre site near downtown Denver. The landforms, structures, and plants are arranged to enclose distinct elements and portions of the garden. They are used to focus and enhance views, and to create backdrops, effects of light and shade, striking and interesting patterns, and a variety of spaces contrasting in activity, size and form. Major tree plantings and other important landscape elements, such as the water system, mounds and depressions, are intended to unify the garden with continuity and emphasis. It is intended that there be no one point from which the entire garden is visually apparent. Rather, the garden is to be experienced as a sequence of pleasant discoveries as one moves along the path.

The Rose Garden provides an important focus for the entire gardens. Water features, raised planters, trellises and arbors, beds, mounds, walkway, walls and spatial enclosure by major plantings provide for roses to be displayed in every conceivable manner within a highly organized architectural framework in Colorado's largest rose garden.

The Fragrance Garden concept stresses the senses of touch, smell and hearing by the use of intimate pathways with raised beds of fragrant plants, while plantings and earth forms create a variety of temperature and light intensity zones which enhance the sensory experience.

The Alpine and Rock Garden is a 3/4-acre specialty garden. The distinct climatic and elevational advantages of Denver provides an opportunity to develop a large collection of plants in a wide variety of natural conditions.

The Morrison Horticultural Demonstration Center is the central focus of the Community Garden Square. The Demonstration Center is designed to communicate concepts in horticultural therapy through user observation and through the demonstration of various types of equipment, plants, work areas, and activities. The design program's main objective was to have the Demonstration Center's garden accessible by all people regardless of age or mental or physical handicap. Centrally located in the garden is the fountain, designed as a central focus and planter for aquatic plants.

Ornamental pool and water cascade.

Rock garden.

Gardens entrance.

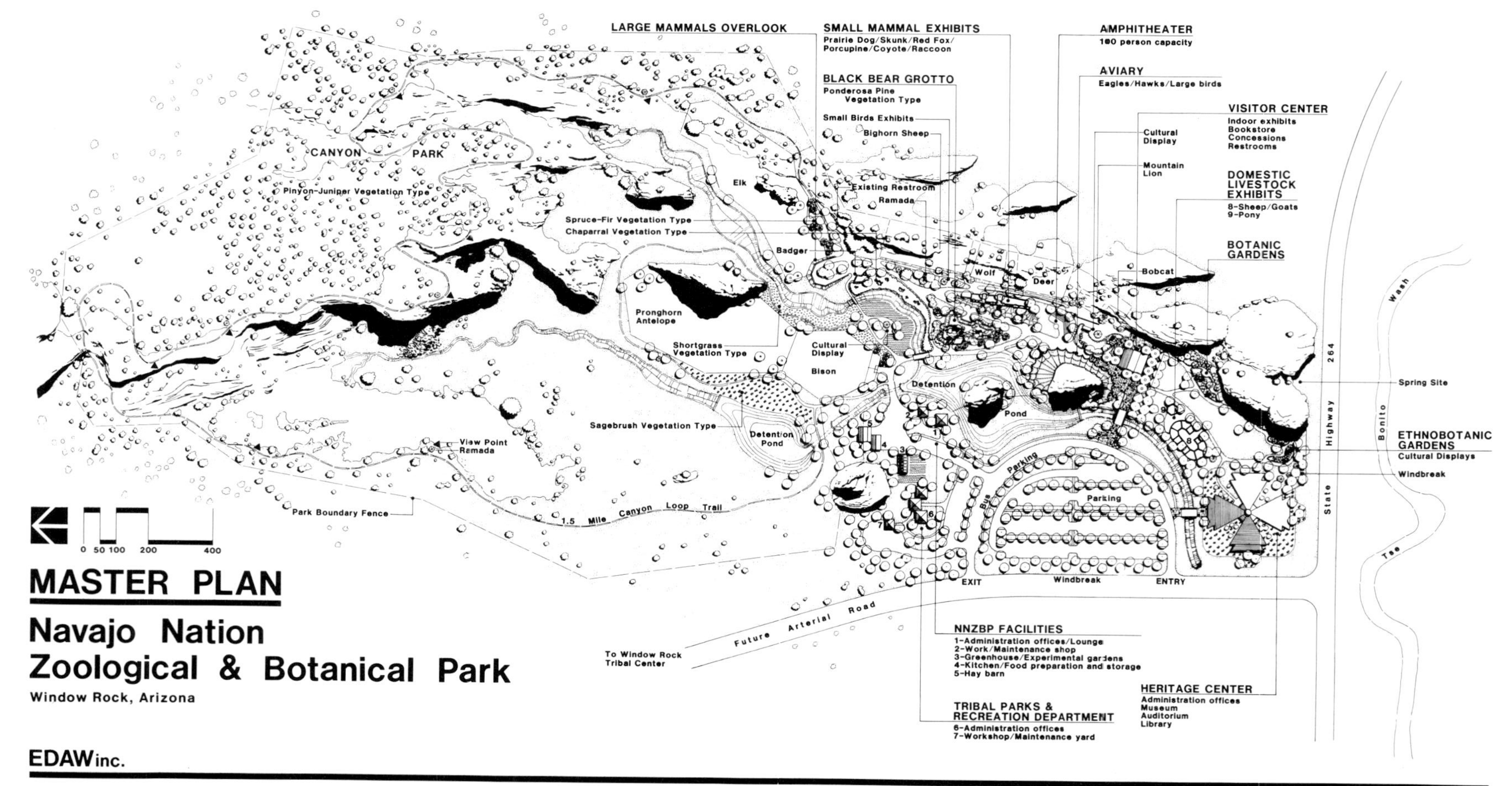

MASTER PLAN

Navajo Nation
Zoological & Botanical Park

Window Rock, Arizona

EDAWinc.

NAVAJO NATION ZOOLOGICAL AND BOTANICAL PARK
Window Rock, Arizona

Design firm: EDAW, Inc.

This park is sited within a scenic red rock area in Window Rock. It is unique among zoos in the southwest in that its primary goal is to collect and exhibit animals and plants historically significant to the Navajo Indian culture. The site is organized into three distinct areas from south to north: (1) domestic animals, ethnobotanic gardens, and picnic area adjacent to the future Cultural/Visitor Center, (2) core exhibit area displaying animals along with their associated habitats, and (3) a large fenced canyon park with interpretive trails where visitors will have the opportunity to learn about the canyon ecosystem and possibly observe deer and pronghorn set free in the area.

Concept sketch of park design and Layout.

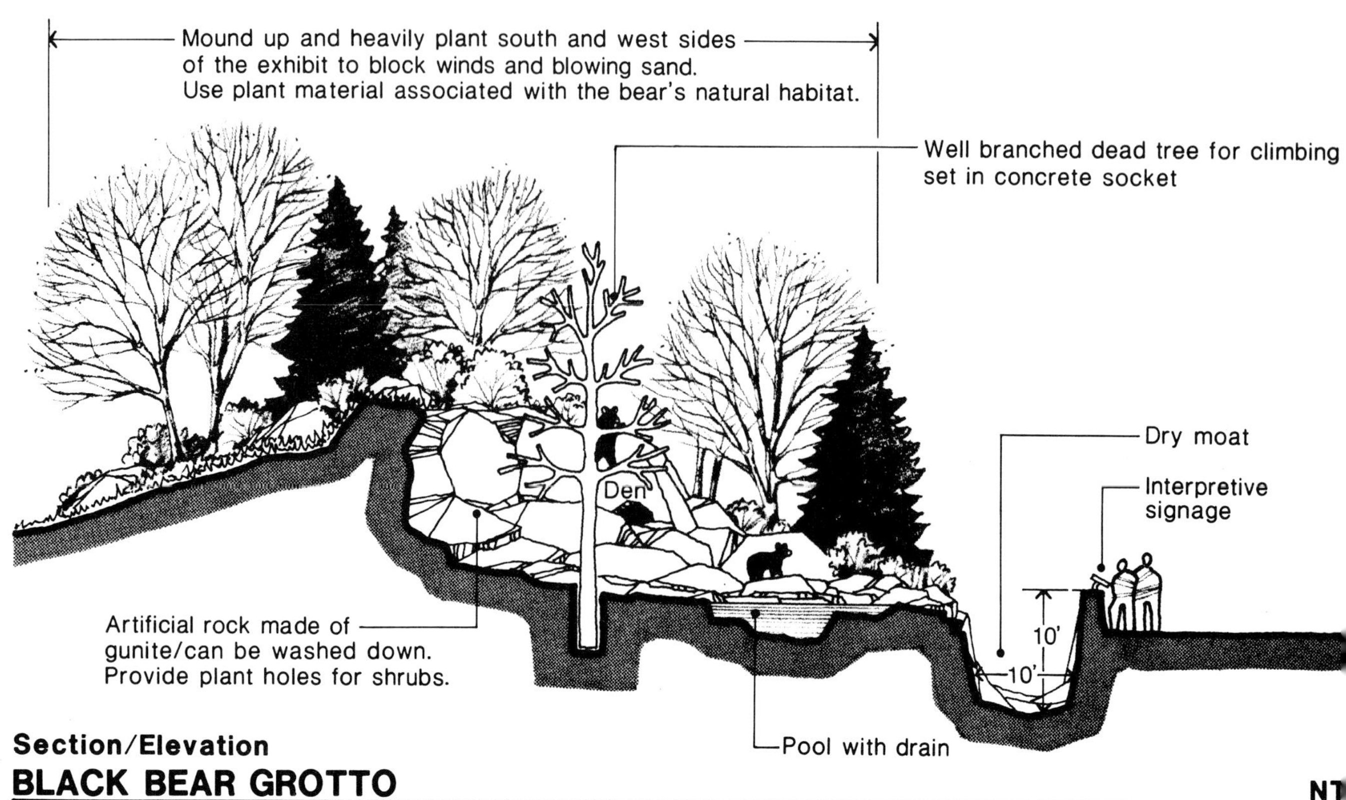

Section/Elevation
BLACK BEAR GROTTO
NT

Section/Elevation
AVIARY/EAGLE EXHIBIT
NT

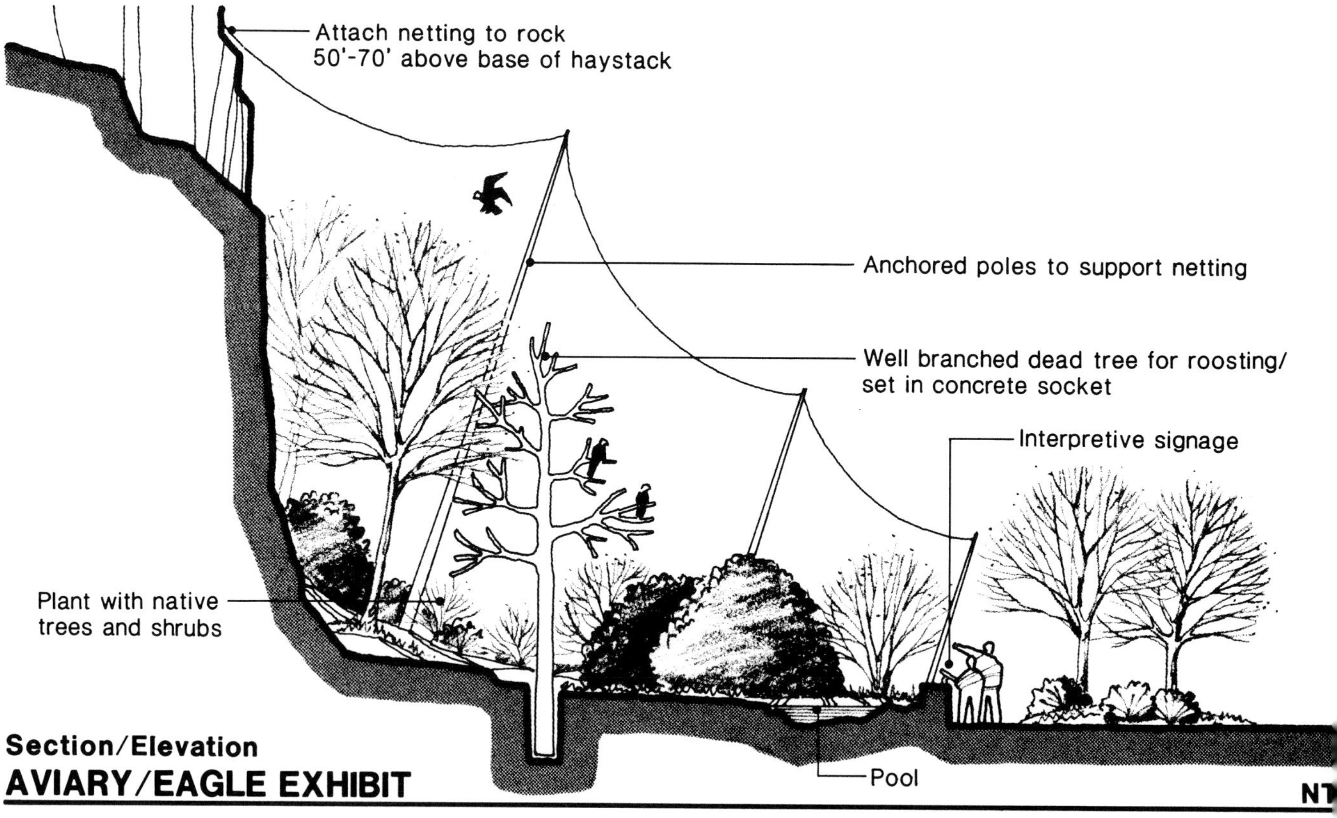

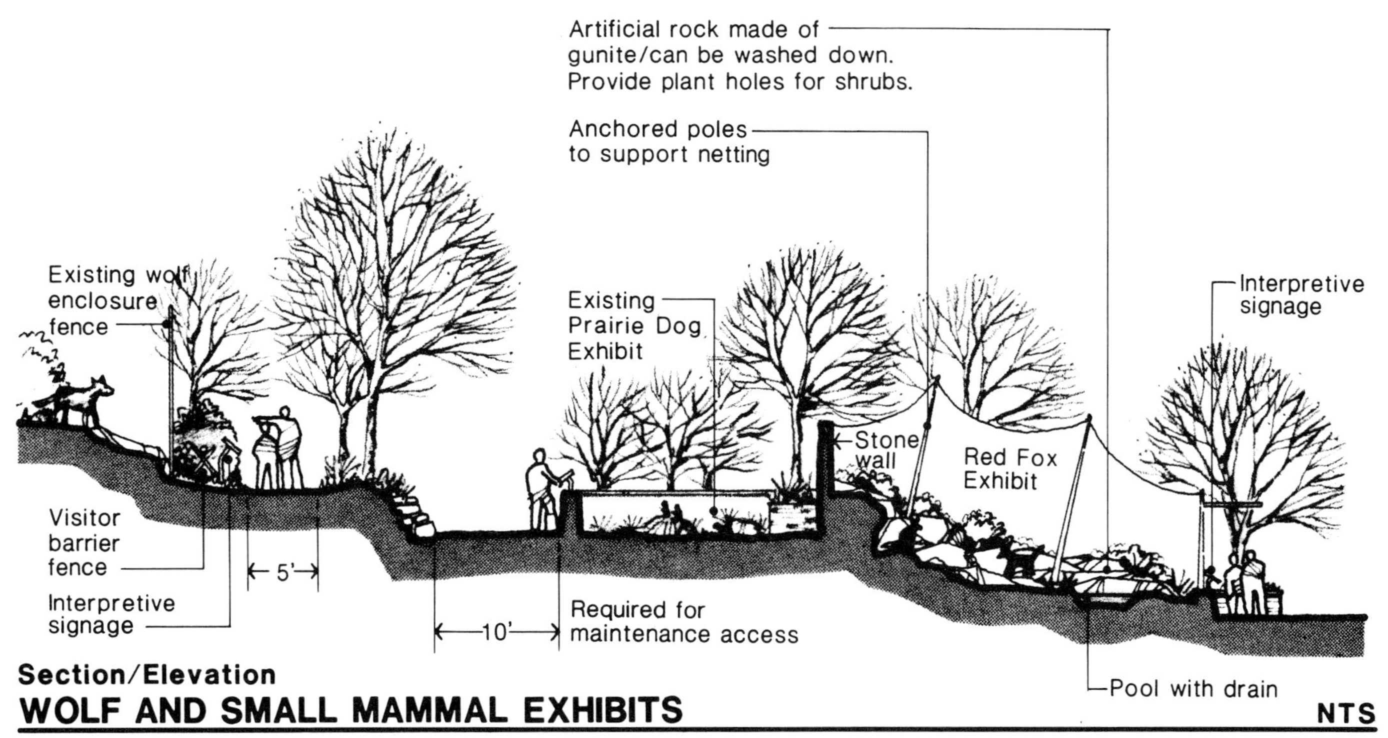

Section/Elevation
WOLF AND SMALL MAMMAL EXHIBITS

NTS

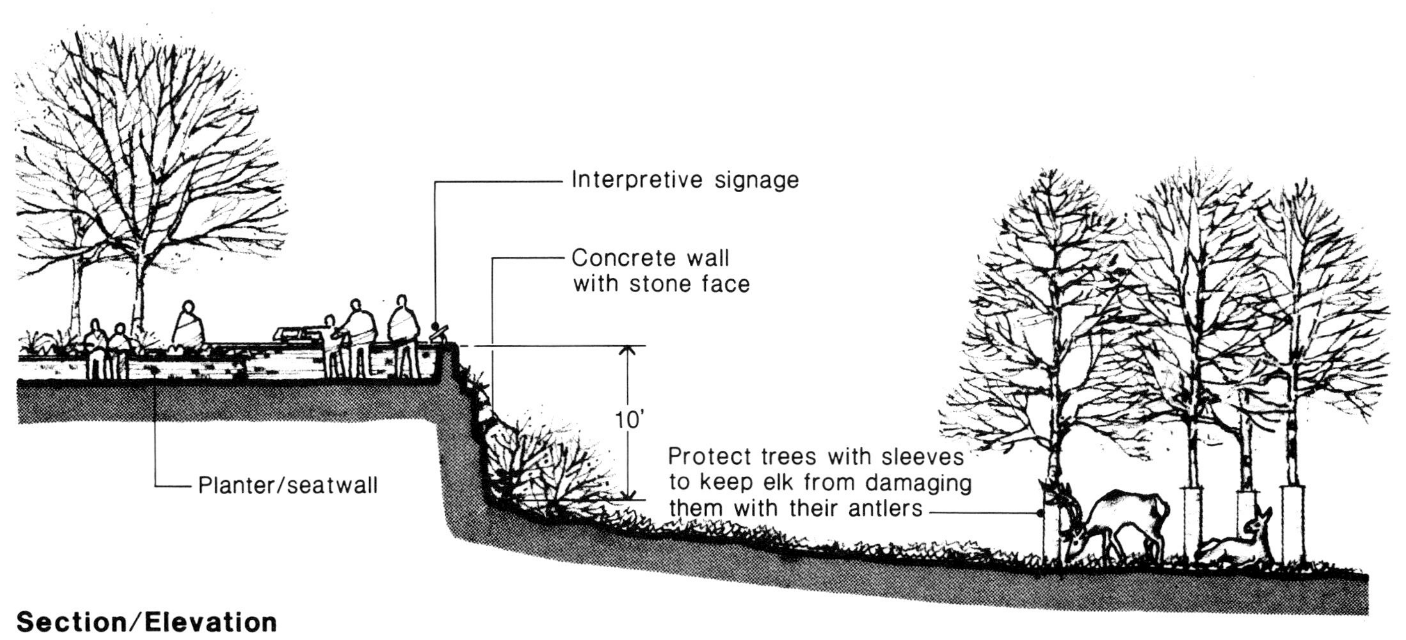

Section/Elevation
LARGE MAMMALS OVERLOOK/ELK ENCLOSURE

NTS

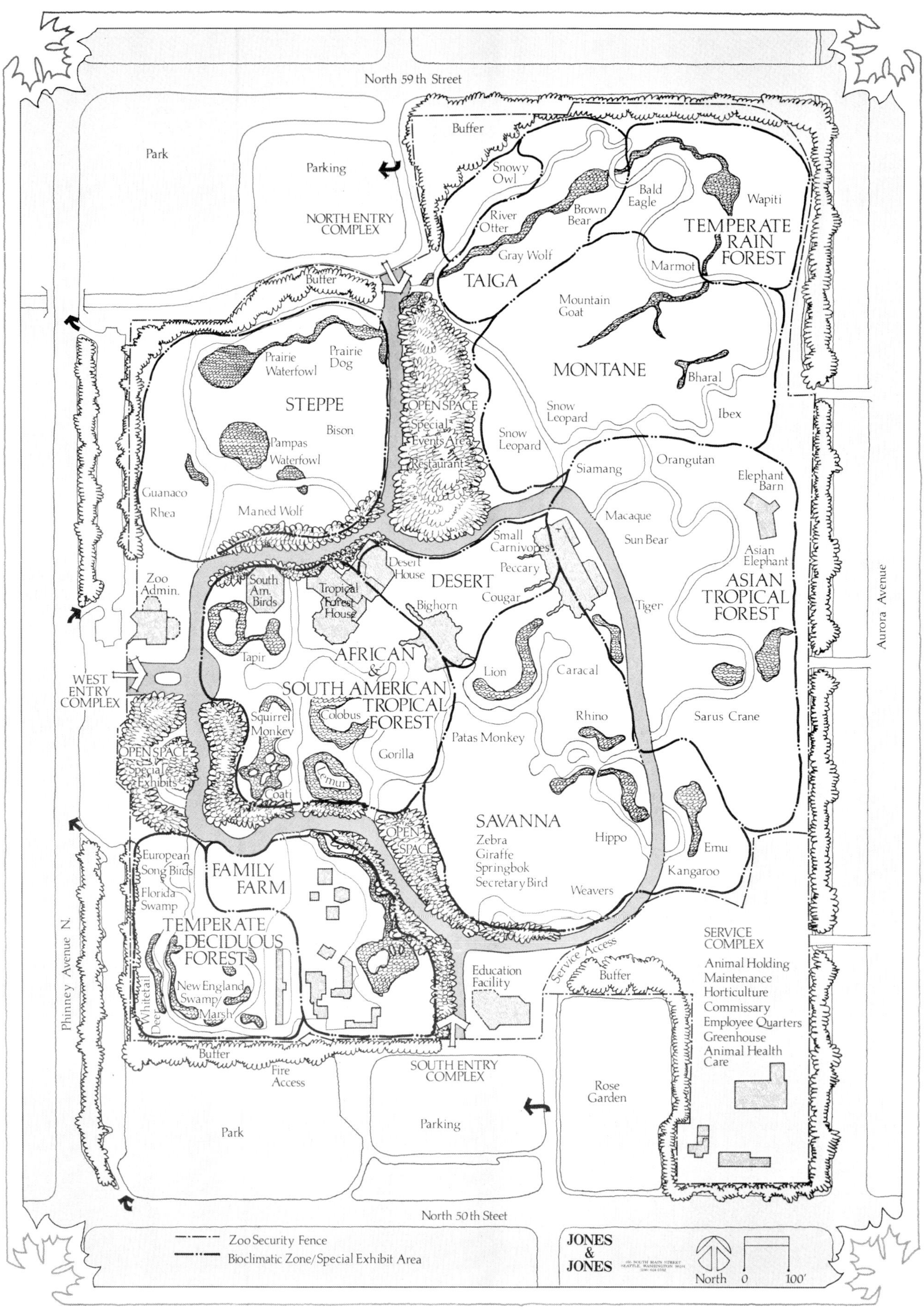

Master Plan for Woodland Park Zoo.

WOODLAND PARK ZOOLOGICAL GARDENS
Seattle, Washington

Design firm: Jones & Jones

A zoo which has benefitted from long range planning and sufficient funding to make it recognized for its great range of technical solutions and innovative concepts for the exhibition of animals. The master plan provides for current as well as longrange development of animal exhibits as well as the visitor and service facilities that support them.

The animal exhibits are organized within bioclimatic zones, corresponding to the special plant formations associated with the world's diverse climates. The zones include Tropical Forest, Savanna, Desert, Steppe, Chaparral, Temperate Deciduous Forest, Temperate Rain Forest, Taiga, Tundra and Montane, each with its own assemblage of animal species.

The bioclimatic zones are further divided into geographic regions, each with its own exhibit complex. Thus, the zoo is organized in the same pattern in which these zones and regions intergrade into one another in nature, so that a trip through the zoo simulates quite accurately a similar trip to the natural regions of the world. Social biology is a secondary theme, augmenting the bioclimatic-zone presentation. Animals are not only kept in naturalistic settings, but live in natural social groupings as in the wild.

Natural animal habitat.

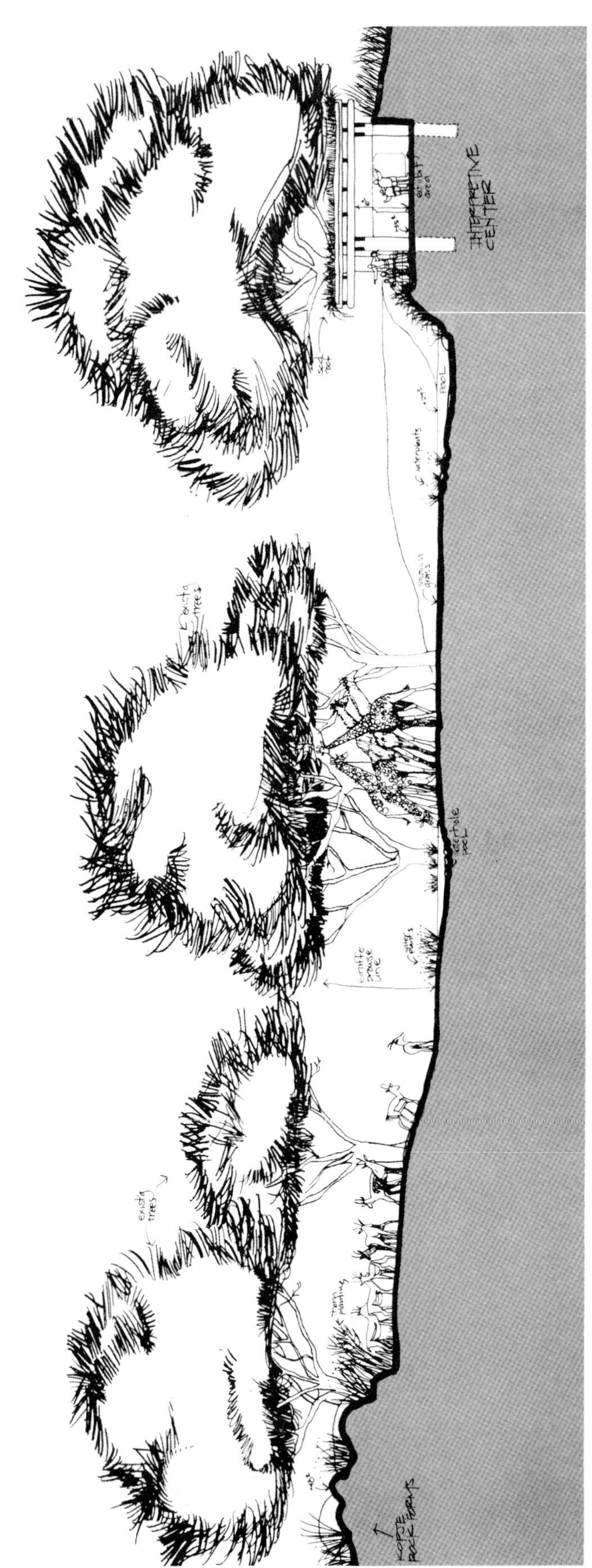

Section through typical animal habitat.

Natural habitats at Woodland Park Zoo.

Animal habitat at Arizona-Sonora Desert Museum.

ARIZONA-SONORA DESERT MUSEUM
Tucson, Arizona

This museum is part of Tucson Mountain Park and is a private non-profit institution. Facilities include an aviary, arboretum of native Arizona plants and cactus, demonstration gardens and numerous animal habitats. The newest habitats have been constructed to simulate the natural habits of the animals on display. Imitation rock is used, but has been designed to blend into the natural desert which is adjacent to the museum.

Entrance to man-made underground cave and display area.

Wolf habitat.

Screened entrance to service area.

Entrance to Aviary at the Arizona-Sonora Desert Museum.

Trail connecting several animal habitats.

Cougar habitat.

Chuckwalla habitat.

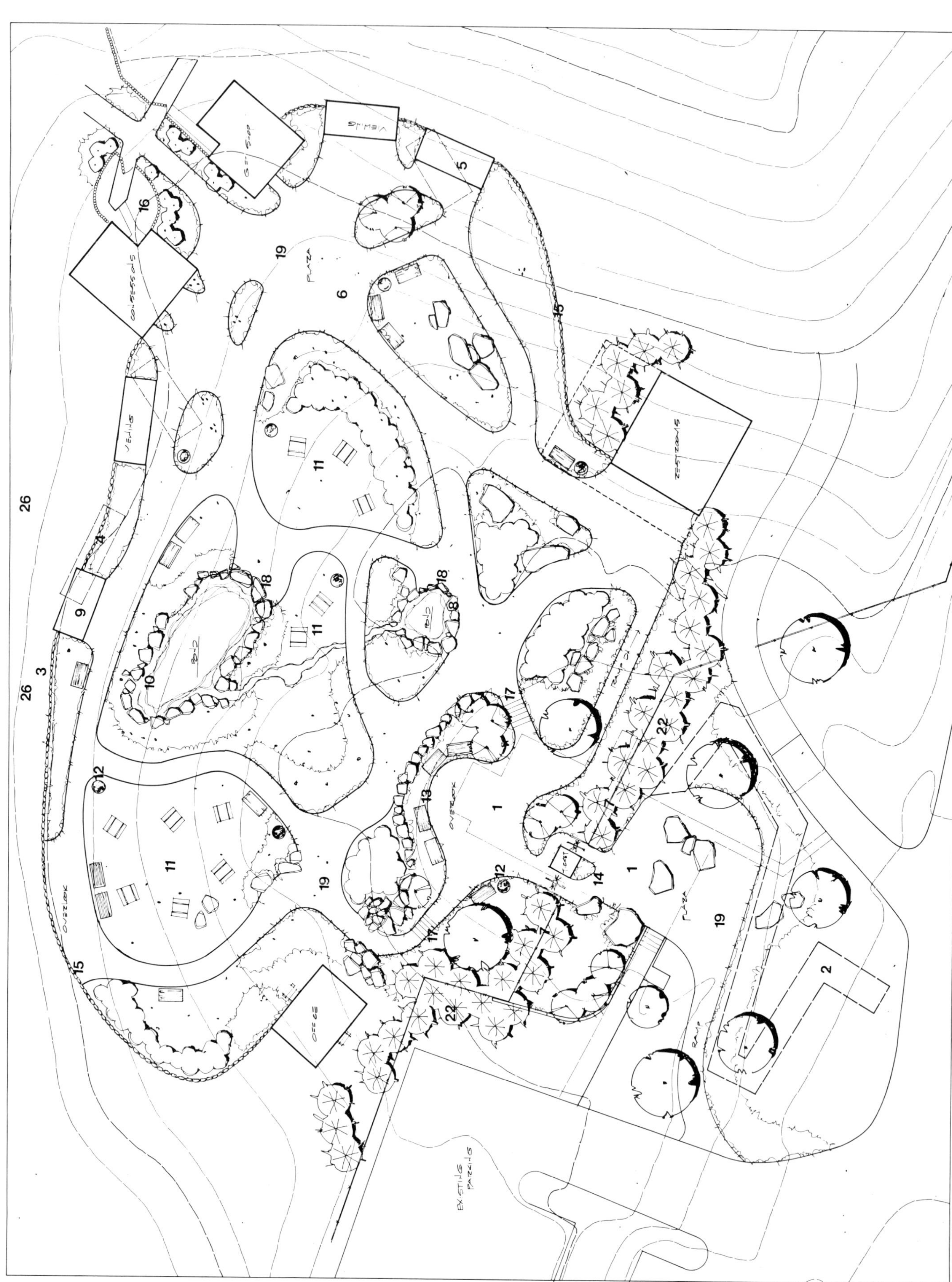

Master Plan for Stone Mountain Animal Forest.

STONE MOUNTAIN ANIMAL FOREST
East Atlanta, Georgia

Design firm: Eberly & Associates

Adjacent to Stone Mountain Park, a large outcropping of solid granite, 100 acres of park land was set aside for this "animal forest." It is a natural habitat for various native American animal species including bison, elk and deer. The existing site consists of rolling terrain with a mix of hardwoods and pine. The portion of the site developed is on high ground allowing viewing into the lower natural habitats. The forest is subdivided by a series of fenced trails for observers to walk and view.

The developed area includes a ticket booth, general office, restroom facilities, two classroom buildings, and four "viewing shelters" as overlooks into the forest. This area is designed to function as a meeting place and holding area for visitors using the trails.

Handicapped access has been provided for this park. Trails are meandering so no trail slope exceeds 8 percent and to preserve the natural grades of the surrounding land. Access from the main park loop road was provided by means of a wood bridge and ramp system.

Two ponds were created within the site by relocating granite boulders nearby. A small pond on the knoll was excavated and connected to a larger lower pond by means of waterflow through a natural swale.

The periphery of the site was defined by use of a low stone wall of native granite and constructed of stone quarried within the park. The wall was designed to both visually contain people and to physically separate the entrance and holding area from the lower animal habitat.

KEY TO NUMBERS ON THE MASTER PLAN

 1. Asphalt plaza and meeting space
 2. Handicap wood ramp access to bridge
 3. Animal control fence location
 4. Relocated shelter
 5. Viewing shelter
 8. Upper pond – water source
 9. Viewing shelter
10. Lower pond and drain
11. Picnic area
12. Trash receptacle
13. Overlook with log benches
14. Ticket booth – access control
15. Stacked granite control wall
16. Service area
17. Concrete steps
18. Replace boulders
19. Asphalt path system
22. White Pine screen
26. Animal territory

Pond with viewing shelter, concession and gift shops.

Sitting area and viewing shelters. Photos by Steve Hogben.

Wood access bridge and ramp system.

Wood trellis at University of Washington Arboretum. Design by Jongejan/Gerrard/McNeal.

MISCELLANEOUS FACILITIES

The photographs which are shown in this section of the book represent a diversity of design ideas and illustrate such facilities as play structures and equipment, picnic shelters, gazebos, arbors, signs, tables, seating, amphitheatres, marinas, bridges, water features, and zoo habitats. Design firms involved with these facilities have been named when they were known.

Wood trellis detail. Design: Belt Collins. Photo: Tom Papandrew.

Trellis at Curtis Park, Dallas.

Trellis and picnic table. Design: Belt Collins. Photo: Tom Papandrew.

Trellis at a park in Cincinnati.

Trellis with a mountain as a focal point. Arizona-Sonora Desert Museum.

Gazebo with culvert. Design: Belt Collins. Photo: Tom Papandrew.

Picnic ramadas at Embarcadero Marina Park, San Diego. Design: Wimmer Yamada Associates.

Boeddeker Park, San Francisco.

Scottsdale, Arizona.

Embarcadero Park, San Francisco.

Fort Lincoln Park, Washington, D.C. Design: M. Paul Friedberg Partners.

Embarcadero Marina Park, San Diego. Design: Wimmer Yamada Associates.

Columbia Park, Seattle.

Near Gene Coulon Park, Renton, Washington.

Jonathan, Minnesota. Design: Bailey & Associates.

Park at Irvine, California.

Cedar Valley College, Dallas. Design: Myrick Newman Dahlberg & Partners.

Santa Cruz River Park, Tucson, Arizona.

Murray City Park, Utah.

Val Vista Lakes Recreation Center, Arizona.

Sun shade for visitors to the Arizona-Sonora Desert Museum.

Circular steel frame and cables to a center ring hold light weight reed screen in position for shade.

Amphitheatre at Purdue University, West Lafayette, Indiana.

Murray City Park, Utah.

Fort Lincoln Park, Washington, D.C. Design: M. Paul Friedberg & Partners.

Play structure and mound at Murray City Park, Utah.

Play structure at Jonathan, Minnesota. Design: Bailey & Associates.

Boeddeker Park, San Francisco.

Boeddeker Park, San Francisco.

All photos from page 214 through page 217 are of Fort Lincoln Park playground in Washington, D.C. Design: M. Paul Friedberg & Partners.

All photos on this page and page 219 are of the playground at SeaWorld in San Diego. Bright colored plastic panels are used throughout.

Oriental style playground in Oakland, California. A concrete dragon circles the play equipment.

Play area at Indian School Park, Indian Bend Wash, Scottsdale, Arizona.

Play structure at the San Francisco Zoo.

Bridge at Fort Lincoln Park, Washington, D.C.

Bridge for bicycle trail at Indian Bend Wash, Scottsdale, Arizona.

Minneapolis Parks. Design: Interdesign Inc.

Gene Coulon Park, Renton, Washington. Design: Jones & Jones.

Japanese Garden in the University of Washington Arboretum, Seattle.

SeaWorld, San Diego.

Hawaii Resort. Design: Belt Collins. Photo: Tom Papandrew.

Tennis court complex. Val Vista Lakes Recreation Center, Arizona.

Circular stone veneer seating for a softball diamond at Murray City Park, Utah.

Tennis court seating for a Hawaii Resort. See adjacent photo on page 227. Design: Belt Collins Associates, Walters Kimura Associates, Tongg Clarke Mechler Associates. Photos by Tom Papandrew.

San Diego waterfront. Design: Kawasaki Theilacker Associates.

Recreation area in Irvine, California.

San Diego waterfront. Design: Kawasaki Theilacker Associates.

Fort Lincoln Park, Washington, D.C.

Fort Lincoln Park, Washington, D.C.

Scottsdale, Arizona.

Cedar River Trail, Renton, Washington. Design: Jongejan/Gerrard/McNeal.

San Diego waterfront. Pedestrian walk in center, road on right, and bicycle path on left separated by planting.

Bicycle parking in San Diego.

Water Gardens in Fort Worth, Texas. Design: Philip Johnson.

Moon Walk, New Orleans, provides pedestrian access to the Mississippi River. Formerly an industrial site.

Recreation Center for a housing development in Mesa, Arizona.

Primate Discovery Center, San Francisco Zoo.

Educational sign, Cincinnati Zoo.

See below.

Signage at Wailea Resort in Hawaii. Design: Belt Collins Associates, Walters Kimura Associates, Tongg Clarke Mechler Associates. Photos by Thomas P. Papandrew.

See bottom of page 234.

San Diego. Design by Wimmer Yamada Associates.

Fairfax County Parks, Virginia.

Showers for Hawaiian beaches. Design: Belt Collins Associates.

Trash enclosure. Belt Collins Associates.

REFERENCES FOR FURTHER READING

Christensen, Monty L. *Park Planning Handbook.* New York: John Wiley, 1977.

Eriksen, Aase. *Playground Design.* New York: Van Nostrand Reinhold, 1986.

Molnar, Donald J., and A. J. Rutledge. *Anatomy of a Park.* 2nd ed. New York: McGraw-Hill, 1986.

INDEX